The Charlton Story

PETER LANG
New York • Washington, D.C./Baltimore • Bern
Frankfurt am Main • Berlin • Brussels • Vienna • Oxford

Earle Perry Charlton II
& George Winius

The Charlton Story

EARLE PERRY CHARLTON, 1863–1930
One of the Five Founders of the F. W. Woolworth Company

PETER LANG
New York • Washington, D.C./Baltimore • Bern
Frankfurt am Main • Berlin • Brussels • Vienna • Oxford

Library of Congress Cataloging-in-Publication Data

Charlton, Earle Perry.
The Charlton story: Earle Perry Charlton, 1863–1930: one of
the five founders of the F. W. Woolworth Co. / Earle Perry Charlton II and George Winius.
p. cm.
Includes bibliographical references.
1. Charlton, Earle Perry, 1863–1930. 2. Businessmen—United States—
Biography. 3. F. W. Woolworth Company. I. Title.
HF5465.U62 C48   381'.12'092—dc21   2001029852
ISBN 0-8204-5558-X (hardcover)
ISBN 0-8204-3927-4 (paperback)

Die Deutsche Bibliothek-CIP-Einheitsaufnahme

Charlton II, Earle Perry:
The Charlton story: Earle Perry Charlton, 1863–1930: one of
the five founders of the F. W. Woolworth Co. / Earle Perry Charlton II and George Winius.
−New York; Washington, D.C./Baltimore; Bern;
Frankfurt am Main; Berlin; Brussels; Vienna; Oxford: Lang.
ISBN 0-8204-5558-X (hardcover)
ISBN 0-8204-3927-4 (paperback)

Cover design by Lisa Dillon

The paper in this book meets the guidelines for permanence and durability
of the Committee on Production Guidelines for Book Longevity
of the Council of Library Resources.

© 2001 Peter Lang Publishing, Inc., New York

Printed in the United States of America

Dedicated to all the people whose lives were touched by the
foresight and brilliance of a great man:
Earle Perry Charlton.

ACKNOWLEDGMENTS

FINDING INDIVIDUALS WHO KNEW E. P. CHARLTON, who died seventy years ago, on November 20, 1930, is difficult if not virtually impossible. Fortunately, the memory of Earle Perry Charlton lives on with many people, particularly in Southeastern Massachusetts because of family ties, his remarkable career in retailing, and what his legacy has meant to people in the present era through philanthropic efforts and the good deeds that have been accomplished in his name.

My profound thanks and gratitude go to the University of Massachusetts Dartmouth for initiating the idea of writing this book about a great man and underwriting the project. I would especially like to thank the former Chancellor, Peter H. Cressy, now in Washington D.C., who spearheaded the writing of this book, along with Benjamin F. Taggie, then Provost at the University of Massachusetts Dartmouth, Ronald D. McNeil, Dean of the Charlton College of Business, and Donald H. Ramsbottom, Executive Director of the University of Massachusetts Dartmouth Foundation who has been a longtime friend of mine and the Charlton family. The present Chancellor of the University of Massachusetts Dartmouth, Jean MacCormack, has continued with her support of this book.

As for individual contributors to this book, I would especially like to thank Robert A. Kerner of San Francisco, whose father, Simon Kapstein, was one of E. P. Charlton's most trusted associates. Bob was kind enough to give us permission to use and quote from Simon Kapstein's unfinished autobiography and this, along with the letters that I was fortunate to find in the Woolworth Regional Office in Burlingame, California, when I was Regional Manager of the Pacific Region, gave us an unusual insight of what went on within the stores in the early 1900s. The letters and all the photographs used in this book have been given to the Archives and Special Collections of the Library of the University of Massachusetts Dartmouth. They constitute part of the Charlton archive and are provided courtesy of the Library and published with my permission.

Mrs. Florence Brigham, curator of the Fall River Historical Society for so many years, until she died at 100 years of age in January 2000, was very helpful in relating stories about Fall River families including the Charltons; her successor, Michael Martins, has done a remarkable job of preserving the history of Fall River and was a great resource to me in obtaining various information. Bill Wyatt and the Westport Historical Society have also been a great source of inspiration to me with their *Pond Meadow* exhibition and a record crowd who were present for a talk and presentation that I gave at the Acoaxet Club during the summer of 2000.

Among my close associates and friends who gave me valuable support and assistance on this book (along with Don Ramsbottom) were Frederic "Rick" C. Dreyer, Jr., former President of Charlton Memorial Hospital, John B. Day, President and CEO of Southcoast Health System, Ronald B. Goodspeed, M.D., President of Southcoast Hospital Group, Sumner James Waring, Jr. whose family have been close personal friends of the Charlton family over many years, and Rev. Dr. Robert P. Lawrence, pastor of the First Congregational Church of Fall River and his wife, Dr. Elizabeth (Betty) Lawrence who were both close friends of both the Charlton and Mitchell families, and Waldo E. Dodge, retired personal banker for the Charlton and Mitchell families.

The Woolworth Company (now called the Venator Group) was less than cooperative when it came to giving out any pertinent historical information. Several attempts were made to review historical material, but to no avail. I am indebted to one person, Jennifer D. Vickery, Manager of Corporate Communications, who was in the midst of cleaning out the offices in the Woolworth Building and was kind enough to ask me if I would be interested in the portrait of Earle Perry Charlton which had hung in the Woolworth Board Room since the merger in 1912, and I enthusiastically said that I would be honored to obtain it so that it could hang in the new Charlton College of Business at the University of Massachusetts Dartmouth. My profound thanks to Jennifer for the portrait, several other photos, and an information book on the Woolworth Company.

Finally, I would like to thank George Winius, a distinguished scholar and co-author of this book, for his devoted work, Richard W. Clement of the University of Kansas for his advice on editorial matters, J. Bunker Clark for his editorial work, and Karen Plunkett-Powell for her outstanding portrayal of the rise and fall of the Woolworth Company in her book *Remembering Woolworths*.

Earle Perry Charlton II
San Francisco
November 2000

CONTENTS

Fig. 1. Earle Perry Charlton
1863–1930

FOREWORD

by

Richard Ward

BUSINESSMEN AND ECONOMISTS have long known that entrepreneurs have unique qualities that define and distinguish their actions and drive toward notable success in whatever ventures they undertake. The best of them apply their pecuniary success not only to self-gratification materially but as well to benefit the lives of others. Cutting through the mystique of the entrepreneur, what follows is a brief insight into how ten human characteristics—identified by the French who gave us the word and the gurus of academe who taught and spread the gospel—applied to the life of Earle P. Charlton. Many of these qualities were certainly exhibited famously in the legendary lives of the likes of John D. Rockefeller, Henry Ford, Andrew Carnegie, J. P. Morgan and other tycoons of the past.

In the modern diverse retail era, such pioneers as J. C. Penny, Sam Walton, Jacob Gimbel, Liz Claiborne, K. Gillette and a host of others, prominently including Earle P. Charlton, exemplified creative and constructive business acumen. Each and all also exhibited, not simply business skill, but the true meaning of this adopted French accolade, the entrepreneur—the intrepid knight of the business world, who forsakes the security of a steady job with an established organization to risk often meager or even borrowed resources on a dream. To each of them, it would be a dream of a business venture based on one's own design and expectation of net gain.

In these respects, Earle P. Charlton was, as defined by scholars, the archetypal complete entrepreneur—in his personality, outlook and actions. He was complete in his dedication in that he projected his interests and concerns beyond the enterprise to the welfare of his employees and the greater community.

Richard Ward is former Dean of the Charlton College of Business, University of Massachusetts Dartmouth.

Regarding his adaptability, note in this story of his life how resourcefully Charlton merged opportunity with luck through Frank Woolworth—the legendary giant of retailing—by adopting his strategy of constantly adjusting to new market conditions, opening stores in several locations in different states, only to move on, when any of these failed, to new promising start-ups elsewhere: no hesitation, no hand wringing anxiety or withdrawal, simply moving on to the next best opportunity. In working with the Woolworths and with his partner Seymour Knox, a cousin to Frank Woolworth (more luck?), Earle Charlton learned to adapt his views and decisions to accommodate compromise and still be decisive in managing the growth and complexity of his business empire.

He was a risk taker. All entrepreneurs by definition take risks—calculated though they may be. For Earle Charlton it was the classic leap of faith of his life in his mid twenties when he left a secure sales position with the Thomas C. Newell Company in Boston, not just to enter a partnership with his retailing soul-mate Seymour Knox, but also to start his first store in Fall River, propose marriage to Ida May Stein of Buffalo and then start a family! These were bold moves, fraught with potential difficulty. Beyond the personal, once well underway, though based emotionally and by choice in the Fall River area, his risk taking nature drove him to extend his store openings across the country, despite the obstacles to long distance management and control. Some of these stores were as distant as Vancouver, Montreal, Los Angeles, San Francisco—all at a time when communication and travel were not as facile or expeditious as today. Further manifestation of his capacity for accepting risk, though essentially and by experience a retailer, was in his launching into the role of industrialist when in 1910 he decided to build the Charlton textile mill in Fall River. This was manufacturing—not merchandising a vast array of consumer products. It was a new field! He was not daunted. He was the entrepreneur exemplar. He took the leap of faith; he took the calculated risk.

Striking out on a risky financial commitment at the age of 26 is a daunting and lonely adventure. A belief in one's own abilities and the confidence in one's goal and strategic business plan is a critical component of success. The young Earle Charlton had such confidence when he started his first store in Fall River, when he teamed up with Seymour Knox to spread his concept of store merchandising, and again when, well into his forties, he plunged into building his own textile mill. That is a salient characteristic of entrepreneurs; they exhibit confidence in the face of imposing hurdles and uncertainty. They also take chances with selection of personnel to carry out the business plan that drives the risk taker's ambition to excel. Earle Charlton put great trust in those he hired to manage his growing scatter of stores around the country; he backed them in their decisions, stood by them when difficulties arose, moved non-performers aside. That takes confidence. The founder of MacDonald's restaurant empire, Ray Kroc, had an answer for the scary uncertainly that lurks in every new venture, as well as after every failure: "press on." Given the complex mix of decisions that faced Earle Charlton regarding store locations, openings, closing of weak performers and bucking the shrewdness of his competitors, he, too, would respond to his doubts by resolving always to "press on." He had confidence in himself.

Eagerness to win is the key for the true entrepreneur. The thrill of putting out a better marketing concept than that of his competitors, whether in retailing or in manufacture of textile goods. Earle was not deterred by fierce competition; on the contrary, as common to his type, it stimulated his creative makeup and motivated him to find the specific business components of success in whatever he undertook. Even as Vice President of F. W. Woolworth Company, which brought him all the trappings of financial and social reward, combined with the freedom to indulge his time in whatever recreation, travel or social revelry he fancied, his, by then, well honed competitive instincts drove him on, in 1910, to organize, finance and create that ambitious 90,000 spindle Charlton textile mill project on Cook Pond, one of the largest at the time in Fall River. He did not need the profits derived therefrom to live the good life; he did not need to divert his focus from the retail field he already knew so well to tackle, for him, a completely new industrial field of battle, that of textile manufacture. What he did need was to express his instincts to press on and to engage competitors on an entirely different playing field, with a mill that was more efficient than theirs. Those were his instincts; the instincts of the entrepreneur. The fact that well-established textile mill owners were already ensconced in the market right under his nose in Fall River and in many sections of every New England state, held no crippling fear for him. He was a competitor and he knew how to win. He was an entrepreneur, and entrepreneurs love to compete.

Entrepreneurs are persuasive. And so was Earle Charlton. Considering all the business decisions and moves he made, he had to be very persuasive with his partner, Seymour Knox, and later with his mentors, the Woolworths. The daily decisions regarding personnel that commanded his attention in his far-flung empire of stores, and again in the decisions on store locations and openings that were his, the decisions on hiring and firing, on moving personnel and promoting them, the decision to launch himself into an additional career involved in building his textile mill, the decision, after being named Director of the Haven and Hartford Railroad in 1923, of investing heavily and calling on others likewise to invest, despite the difficult financial straits that particular railroad company was in. All of these areas of his decision making must have required great persuasive skills from Earle Charlton in dealing with his colleagues and partners. One has to assume that the success of the actions that followed contributed to his partners' acceptance of the moves he chose to make. His confidence in the face of risks and competition led to firm decision-making by Earle, which in turn led to repeated successful ventures and company growth. All of this in turn made him a persuasive businessman. This is how entrepreneurs are made.

Can anyone gain leadership and enduring success without this quality? We have to suppose one can, and some do, but not good entrepreneurs. Entrepreneurship as a concept of business practice assumes a high level of integrity. Like his father James Charlton, "one of Chester's (Conn.) most trusted citizens," Earle Charlton was an honest man. His partners trusted him, his employees trusted his demonstrable concern for them, his community acknowledged his desire to use his wealth to soften the harshness of existence for the many. In the innumerable day-to-day exchanges that took place throughout his business career, though when necessary for management stern and judgmental, he bore an open and truthful countenance. He dealt with others eye to eye. And this quality of directness and openness was acknowledged and appreciated by his equals and by those who depended on his decisions for their livelihood and opportunity for advancement and security. It was widely recognized from the pattern of his professional life that it could be said of Earle Charlton that "all of his money was earned honestly and without hindrance to others."

Focus on money alone is not enough, whatever the life endeavor. An entrepreneur, however goal oriented or driven, cannot escape this truism. As in other pursuits, every catalyst of the business world needs a vision.

Even as a young man of twenty six, having just established his first store with Seymour Knox in Fall River, Earle envisioned the expansion of his retail-chain model to Canada and the Far West: mass marketing of an array of merchandise at bargain prices. To him *status quo* was Latin for personal timidity and eventual commercial demise. He also peered confidently into the future and saw the great promise of the 5 and 10 cent concept in the mass moving of goods into the hands of receptive and satisfied consumers.

Though devoted to the environment of his home town of Fall River, Massachusetts—and even reluctant to be away from the region too long—his mind all the while, on the contrary, was on the far horizons and on the promise his business associates, like the Woolworths, recognized as beckoning across the continent, and even beyond its borders. Vision is a common trait to be found in the entrepreneurial make up; it was innately manifested in the behavior of Earle P. Charlton.

To engage in any business venture without assessing the prospect of failure and how you would avert it or react to it would be a serious omission from any business plan. Many successful entrepreneurs get started without resources of their own and without a college education. They have dreams, drive and determination to pursue those dreams. They also have grit. With or without a business plan, entrepreneurs seem instinctively to respond to adversity by "pressing on." Like the response on the other end of the modern business phone, they cultivate options; they activate their "positive thinking" button, and when an effort fails, they put into operation another start up, another project, another "promising opportunity."

Henry Ford failed in a number of enterprises before finding his breakthrough to success. He once said, "failure is a chance to begin again more intelligently. It is just a resting-place. We learn more from our failures than our successes." Again, Earle Charlton fits the entrepreneurial mold. As the accompanying text reveals of Frank Woolworth, "his ultimately successful innovations were not gained without several years of pratfalls. It was not until he had failed several times that he opened a successful and prototypical store in the Amish country of Lancaster, Pennsylvania." Earle Charlton, too, had his "pratfalls." Whether his problems were financial, logistical or with personnel, Earle patiently and determinedly persevered over adversity to get the job done right. This takes long hours and just plain steady, hard work.

Even at the height of his financial success, as the text herein tells us, "he neither paused to loaf and admire his achievements, nor to work repetitively at familiar tasks," but remained committed to action and involvement in a dizzying agenda of "dozens of new activities"—commercial, social, philanthropic.

The worst entrepreneurial models portray individuals of narrow purpose and mean spiritedness. As Christopher Lasch once put it, the narcissistic personality of our time "has little capacity for personal intimacy or social commitment; he feels little loyalty even to the company for which he works." Earle Charlton was not one of these. His trustworthiness and loyalty to his partners and colleagues in the retail empire he helped to build was exemplary. Also, his humane handling of employees, amply recorded in this document, reveals a sensitive and patient loyalty to his store managers and employees and their families. The anecdote concerning the difficulties of Williams, a young store manager in the Butte, Montana store circa 1911, portrays Earle as an executive of abundant compassion. He would not fire the young man based on his mistakes, nor on questionable evidence or hearsay.

Similarly, his sensitivity to human predicament was evidenced again in the saga of poor Louis Perini, Frank Woolworth's valet, who had been ignored in Woolworth's will and faced, it appeared, almost certain prospect of joblessness and consequent return to his native Italy. Learning of this, Earle Charlton notified the man that he was forthwith hired to be his personal valet at his Westport Pond Meadow estate, where he remained for the next sixty years!

It goes without question that in his personal life, Earle loved his family relationships, particularly his grandchildren, and relished the company and numerous activities he indulged in with all of them.

Add to these cameo views of Earle's character—keeping in mind how occupied he was with his daily business affairs—consider the "humanizing, constructive and positive" role the Charlton and Woolworth stores played in our society. They were user-friendly by design in terms of size, stability and attentiveness of the employees to consumer needs, as well as affordable in pricing policy. These are features that reflected an understanding company culture, fostered by both Earle Charlton and Frank Woolworth.

People will often be judged and sometimes redeemed by what they leave behind. Not all entrepreneurs conform to predicable attributes of either asceticism or profligacy when it comes to use of their prodigious wealth. Stories of the pinchpenny ways of Henry Ford Sr., John D. Rockefeller and Andrew Carnegie in their early years and even, to some extent, in their primes are legendary, each having struggled with poverty when young. One tale is told, possibly apocryphal, of a visit by Henry Ford Sr. to Ireland when he was pressed to contribute to the country's hospital fund campaign. Finally yielding, perhaps given his reputation reluctantly, to the widely publicized notoriety of his presence in the land, he coughed up $5,000 for the cause. The next day, the bold headline in the newspaper proclaimed, "FORD GIVES $50,000 TO HOSPITALS." Confronting his hosts in some agitation the next morning, Ford remonstrated, "But my gift was for $5,000!" To which the clever response was, "Mr. Ford, we are embarrassed and terribly sorry about that error. We intend to correct that mistake in tomorrow's headlines." The outcome is predictable. Whether factual or not, it was only through such wiles, Ford's life reveals, that he could be cajoled into being personally generous, though his enormous wealth was posthumously liberally distributed through his charities and foundations. Unlike Henry Ford or John D. Rockefeller, Earle Charlton was no ascetic in his personal lifestyle. He enjoyed his wealth to the fullest. He had his mansions and sumptuous abodes in Fall River, Acoxet, Palm Beach and elsewhere, his cadres of servants, including his personal valet Perini, his four yachts, his love of good food, travel, golf, his absorbing hobby of showing his dog Asko at regional, national and international dog shows, and all the other pleasurable social and entertaining outlets any human being could want.

Yet, the record shows clearly that Earle was truly a generous man— to his employees, to numerous specific charities and to the communities where he lived and worked. In effect, he was the prototypical good entrepreneur, as Andrew Carnegie became later in life, having acquired his huge fortune. Unable to find steady work in Scotland, Andrew's father brought the family to Pittsburgh, where Andrew found his first job as a lowly bobbin boy in a cotton mill. Poverty and hard work were the proving grounds for the Carnegie will to strive and succeed. In time, with consummate financial success his reward, he turned to philanthropy, believing that rich men were "trustees" of their wealth to be used for the common good. We know the rest of the Carnegie story: 2,800 libraries, Carnegie Hall, Carnegie Foundation for Teaching, Carnegie Foundation for International Peace, contributions to many other causes. Yet, though without so much notoriety, in proportion to his own wealth, it is said that Earle Charlton gave away as much as did Rockefeller, Ford and Carnegie through their Foundations—an empathetic generosity, as the historian Jacque Barzun has observed of history, not universally demonstrated in the actions of contemporary multi-millionaires and billionaires.

Besides caring amply for his heirs and contributing to furthering his favorite political figures, Earle Charlton could feel comfortable that he might well be favorably judged and perhaps redeemed—despite the affluence reflected in his lifestyle—based on the quality of his extensive philanthropic programs, many carried out through trusts he left behind to reflect his "charitable impulses": multiply these dollar figures by at least twenty to gain comparable generosity in today's dollars—the initial $500,000 gift in 1926 to the Truesdale Hospital in Fall River, then "the largest contribution ever made to any institution in New England," combined with many smaller grants for other special hospital rooms, ambulances, and equipment. Years later, in 1979, the Charlton Charitable Trust he left behind would grant another $1,000,000 to facilitate the merging of Truesdale and Union Hospitals in Fall River, and support liberally dozens of other causes in Fall River alone, all detailed in the account to follow in this book.

- $110,000 to the Clarke School for the Deaf.
- $50,000 to the New England Medical Center in Boston.
- Six major contributions, well into the millions of dollars, to the Mayo Clinic made by Earle's eldest daughter, Ruth (who had married a Mayo physician following the death of her first husband), for buildings, scholarships, research, equipment.
- Carrying on the noble philanthropic tradition of his grandfather, his namesake and grandson Earle P. ("Chuck") Charlton II in 1999 granted, among his other charitable works, $3,000,000 to the College of Business at the University of Massachusetts Dartmouth, now known as, the Charlton College of Business.

Not to overelaborate on the tale to follow, the above list is greatly abbreviated in its detail of Earle Charlton's on-going philanthropic legacy, imparting to untold thousands of human beings, now and in future, who have been and will be uplifted in so many ways—educationally, physically, medically, financially, emotionally, recreationally—because "his impulse to alleviate the suffering of others ran so deep."

Taking the full measure of the man, his life and his legacy through his family trusts, Earle Charlton was the quintessential entrepreneur. By sheer hard labor, grit, independence of mind and determination, he rose from the meager lifestyle of a blacksmith's son through contrary career choices, to sharp focus on goals to achieve in retailing, through humane executive skill to phenomenal financial success, wealth, happiness, cultivation of family, and finally to full expression of those "charitable impulses." He exhibited the textbook characteristics of the entrepreneur to reach the pinnacle of every businessperson's dreams, but he did it with humanity and sensitivity to the trials and sufferings of others less fortunate. The same could not confidently be said for the John Jacob Astors, Hetty Greens, Jay Goulds, or even the Frank Woolworths. As a friend of Earle Charlton, Frank Woolworth was a partner to respect, to learn from. Yet, Woolworth left virtually all of his fortune to his family, which in the end wound up as $50 million in his granddaughter Barbara Hutton's keeping, to her ruination, alas, finally forming in her "a recluse, lonely and almost penniless." Woolworth's entrepreneurial dream was not capstoned with a legacy of humane philanthropy, such as we find emblazoned on the plaques for Andrew Carnegie, Ford, Rockefeller, or, let it be said on this record of his life, for Earle P. Charlton.

INTRODUCTION

And when at last, far hence the day,
From earth his name shall fade away
Proudly the heavenly streets we'll stray
In haloes bought at Charlton's!

— Fall River *Globe*, 29 February 1908,
in celebration of the E. P. Charlton
Company's 18th anniversary.

THE HISTORY OF AMERICAN RETAIL BUSINESS has until recently gone largely unstudied, at least in contrast to that of the great financial and manufacturing barons of the late nineteenth and early twentieth centuries: Andrew Carnegie, J. P. Morgan, and Henry Ford have had thousands of pages written about them, while a figure like Frank Woolworth has received very little attention (save for three earlier works, and a more substantial recent popular treatment focussed primarily on the chain itself).[1] Yet retail chains are the most prominent features of the landscape in the United States: every shopping center has its K-Mart or Wal-Mart, its Sears, Dillard's, Walgreen's, Ross, TJ Maxx, Office Depot, Staples, and a host of others. It would seem as if they had always existed, while in fact they are barely older than the twentieth century.

This book is about Earle Perry Charlton (1863–1930), of Fall River, Massachusetts, the associate and friend of Frank W. Woolworth, and an important early figure in the retail chain movement. In contrast to the history of political parties and wars, that of business typically revolves around biography, if because politics and wars are born of interactions between peoples, while commercial movements are typically the work of individuals. Of these, Charlton and his associates, Seymour H. Knox

---

[1] Karen Plunkett-Powell, *Remembering Woolworth's* (New York: St. Martin's Press, 1999). The earlier volumes are James Brough, *The Woolworths* (New York: McGraw-Hill, 1982), John P. Nichols, *Skyline Queen and the Merchant Prince: The Woolworth Story* (New York: Trident Press, 1973), and John K. Winkler, *Five and Ten: The Fabulous Life of F. W. Woolworth*, revised edition (New York: Bantam Books, 1957).

(1861–1915), Frank W. Woolworth (1852–1919), Charles Sumner Woolworth (1856–1947), Fred M. Kirby (1861–1940), and William H. Moore (1841–1916), established the operating principles and norms of chain store operation and were perhaps the first to run them at great distances using only a secretary, a typewriter, postage stamps, and an occasional telegram or telephone call. To offset their lack of sophisticated office equipment they applied perception and vigilance. They were men who kept intimate contact with their subordinates and for whom no detail was too minute. Charlton's fifty-three retail stores in fact spanned North America, yet he preferred to run his company from his desk on South Main Street in Fall River.

His sale of these stores in 1912 was part of a vast amalgamation by Frank Woolworth, one which included not only the Charlton stores, but 543 others, owned by Woolworth and his "family," who thereupon became associates and vice-presidents of the Woolworth corporation and shared in his profits; at Charlton's death his estate was valued at $32,000,000. After his merger with Woolworth, Charlton withdrew from day-to-day operations of the Woolworth chain, but entrained to New York for periodic meetings of its board. Now independently wealthy at the relatively early age of forty-eight, he developed an entirely different side of his nature: that of industrialist, philanthropist, public servant, builder, and clubman—this in contrast to Woolworth who, aside from gourmandise, seems to have possessed few interests outside his empire.

The following chapters discuss his rise to prominence as a businessman, his methods of operation, and his contractual and personal relations with his associates. They describe his manifold activities, family relations and charitable projects. Taken together, these reveal him not only as a pioneer of American retail business, but as a public-minded benefactor reminiscent (though on a smaller scale) of his contemporary, Andrew Carnegie, if indeed without Carnegie's darker sides.

I

THE MERCHANT PRINCE
FROM FALL RIVER

EARLE PERRY CHARLTON was born at Chester, Connecticut, on 19 June 1863, just ten days before the battle of Gettysburg—in other words, at the close of one era and the beginning of a promising new one. Both of his parents were of old New England stock. His father, James D. Charlton, a blacksmith, and his mother, the former Lydia Ladd, were descendants of early New England pioneers and related to the Revolutionary pamphleteer James Otis. The Charltons in fact had emigrated from England in 1636 on the ship *Mary and John,* and first settled in Windsor, a village near Hartford. Earle had two siblings, John Howard, eleven years his senior, and a sister, Mary.[1] Until Earle left home in 1880, his family had moved less than forty miles down the Connecticut River in a little over two centuries.

The forging of hinges, wagon fittings, pitchforks, and horseshoes could scarcely have made the upright and practical James Charlton among the wealthiest citizens of Chester. But whether or not he worked under a Chestnut tree as in Longfellow's poem "The Village Blacksmith," it is virtually certain that, like the poet's own blacksmithing ancestor, he was one of Chester's most trusted citizens and knew everything about his townsmen and surroundings. Perhaps, as well, it was his father's emphasis on the practical above the theoretical that made the youthful Earle leave high school before graduation.[2] But then he

---

[1] Mary married E. A. Bardol, who became Earle's vice-president and right-hand man. After the merger, Bardol joined Woolworth in various capacities and ended his career as a vice-president of that corporation.

[2] Only about one in six enrollees actually completed high school at this period, and its diploma was not considered necessary for success in business.

broke with family artisan tradition and set out to make his living in a wider world.

He already had prepared himself for independence by earning money around Chester as an errand and paperboy, a cattle drover, and almost certainly as part-time clerk in a village store. At any rate, he was determined to become a merchant rather than pursuing his father's trade. It is of course possible that the two clashed temperamentally, but such an explanation for the youthful Earle's failure to follow in his father's footsteps is hardly necessary: blacksmithing was a limited pursuit, and ambitious people of the time must have sensed that their futures could better be served through availing themselves of the great technological changes taking place in American (and European) business than by following old-fashioned village life.

Ever since the dawn of civilization, merchants have comprised that segment of the population who literally thrive on distances, if because the acquisition of something where it can be bought cheaply and its transport to where it can be sold profitably is the essence, and simplest, definition of mercantile activity. In the years after the Civil War, however, the velocity of business accelerated dramatically through improved transport and exchange of information. It is almost a cliché that wars are invariably followed by quickened innovation and change, and the years 1861–65 vastly accelerated the development of two recent technological complexes: the telegraph and the railroad, not to mention the universalizing of mass production and its concomitant interchangeability of parts. Finished products of all sorts could now be ordered by wire, transported virtually overnight, and find markets across great distances; far fewer items, from horseshoes to furniture to clothing, needed to be fabricated locally. Thus, blacksmithing as a way of life must hardly have seemed attractive to an ambitious and intuitive lad like Earle. Around 1878, he left Chester for Hartford, where he worked at a retail store on Asylum Street. In 1880, he migrated to Boston and never returned to live in Connecticut again.

Upon arrival in Boston, he became a clerk and later an ace "drummer," a traveling salesman, for Thomas C. Newell, a distributor of pots, pans, and window accessories whose territory extended throughout

New England and New York.[3] The young man remained with Newell's company for eight years, or until his mid-twenties, traveling its territory and making contacts with Newell's established and prospective clients, lugging and shipping his trunks and boxes of merchandise by train, wagon, and even by boat on the Erie Canal.[4] In the course of these journeys he met his future partner, Seymour Knox, and possibly the brothers Frank and Charles Woolworth as well. To judge from his partnership with Knox, it is probable the young Charlton first sold Newell's merchandise to him as a visiting salesman in his store in Buffalo, but it could even be that he rather met Knox socially, as in a church or a restaurant, or even in a Masonic Lodge.[5] At any rate, the two became friends, and in 1889 Charlton took his first step into the field of five-and-ten retailing with Knox as his partner.

In the years he had worked for Newell, Earle was able to save several hundred dollars, and when he formed his partnership with Knox this nest egg proved adequate for his half-payment on rental property and his share of the new store's merchandise. As events amply came to verify, his meeting with Knox was even more than advantageous, it was serendipitous. Knox was not only an exceptionally kind and able man, but also a first cousin to Frank Winfield Woolworth. In attracting the favorable attention of Knox, unbeknownst to himself, Earle had landed in the best possible matrix for his own considerable talents. To illustrate this, in the next paragraphs we will digress to show what Frank Woolworth had been doing in the years immediately preceding. Then it can be seen that, though temporary, Earle's fortuitous partnership with Knox served him in excellent stead. Not only could he draw upon his new partner's experience for the short run, but it brought him via Knox into what developed into a happy association with Frank Woolworth himself.

---

[3] The Thomas C. Newell Co. was a pioneer in the curtain rod and window accessories business and became the largest wholesale window accessory company in the world. It supplied the F. W. Woolworth Co. with window accessories for over a century.

[4] The *Encyclopedia of American Biography* states that while in the employment of Newell, Charlton was "immediately and conspicuously successful and quickly acquired the reputation as one of the most brilliant salesmen in the United States."

[5] Both he and Knox were Freemasons. Charlton eventually attained the 32nd degree.

FRANK WOOLWORTH AND PARTNERS:
THE PRINCIPLE OF THE FIVE-AND-TEN UNFOLDS

In the same year that Earle teamed with Knox in the formation of a new store, Frank Woolworth was well on his way toward perfecting the five-and-ten-cent store concept. He had come to learn both where to establish new stores and what merchandise to stock in them. His insight was the result of stubborn and repeated efforts, based on trial and error made from the early 1870s. As boys in upstate New York, both he and his younger brother, Charles Sumner Woolworth, had labored from dawn to dusk on their father's farm and were eager to make their mark at something less hard-scrabble and far more rewarding. As the elder of the two, Frank was first to leave the soil and managed to find a rank beginner's job eleven miles away at a prosperous dry goods store called Augsbury and Moore's in Watertown. Although Frank was duly grateful for the opportunity, he received no pay during his first three months he worked as a stock boy and tried his hand (though ineptly) at sales. But he found his *métier* at window-trimming, and his employer, William Moore, not only retained him but also gave him a weekly salary of $3.50. Before long, Woolworth had become familiar with retailing methods of the day and begun to realize where the opportunities lay for innovation.

Augsbury and Moore's layout may be taken as typical of retailing in the earlier nineteenth century, and in fact a few rural hardware and crossroads general stores in the eastern United States still follow the pattern. Smaller items were kept hidden in bins and drawers behind long counters, while larger items were displayed on shelving or concealed in still other drawers along walls behind the counters. There was thus no inspection of merchandise without first waiting one's turn and calling for the help of a salesperson, as "Do you have a pincushion?" or "Have you got a skein of number 44 cotton darning yarn?" or "I see you have lavender chintz, but I need something in light blue." There was thus little or no opportunity to inspect merchandise not already in sight, much less to determine beforehand whether the quality was suitable or the price attractive enough. Nor could one realize an unperceived need when there was so little to inspect. Then there was another difficulty: in addition to the inconvenient way in which merchandise was displayed, people were strapped for disposable income and they may have been reluctant to engage the attention of a salesperson when they feared what they might be shown would prove too expensive.

In the wake of the American Civil War, as in all such widespread and prolonged conflicts, there ensued a surge in prices followed only slowly by a commensurate one in wages. Hence, most people of the lower and middle classes could not afford such luxuries as they had before 1861, but were forced to satisfy their needs with as little outlay as possible. In evolving his response to these circumstances, Frank Woolworth first hit upon the idea of displaying low-cost merchandise purchased in job lots on a special table in his employer's store; later he experimented with renting separate commercial space expressly for such items. It is easy to perceive more than a century later that the five-and-ten idea was beginning to dawn upon him, but his ultimately successful innovations were not gained without several years of pratfalls. It was not until he had failed several times that he opened a successful and prototypical store in the Amish country, in Lancaster, Penn.

By then it was 1879, and he quickly determined to open additional stores in other locations. He thus summoned brother Charles to help him, who meanwhile had left the farm and was managing a branch establishment at Morristown, N.Y., on behalf of another employer. Frank's new location was to be at Harrisburg, Penn. But this store also failed; undaunted, he had Charles open another at York. But while the Lancaster store continued to thrive, York also went under and Charles returned to his old employer. One reason, incidentally, for the failure of these businesses was that Woolworth experimented with stores where everything was uniformly priced at 25¢ rather than containing a mixture of cheaper merchandise. It was only when Frank tried combining goods priced exclusively at 5¢ and 10¢ per item that the subsequent openings of newer stores succeeded. Charles thus returned to Frank's employment, and not only he, but also cousins Seymour H. Knox and Edwin McBrier, joined them to manage stores in other locations. As still more stores opened, those among Frank's trusted managers or bookkeepers, such as Carson Peck and Fred M. Kirby, joined Frank Woolworth, not as employees *per se* but in partnership associations with him or with still other partners. There ensued a whole new string of five-and-tens in which partners each put up half the money.

At this stage, Frank Woolworth did not insist that he or even his kinsmen should enjoy plenary ownership in the growing enterprise or, more properly, loosely interlocking numbers of them. One reason for this was that by 1888 Frank Woolworth was less bent upon owning every store personally than he was upon expanding his collective power to make mass purchases from suppliers, something that enabled him to stock his emporia at lower prices than could his growing number of non-affiliated imitators, and hence achieve the greatest volume and profit among his own and his associated stores in many cities. Thus, he did not object when, in 1889, Seymour Knox, and even his own brother Charles, struck out on their own to open new five-and-tens with himself or others as their partners, while all of them retained their mutual advantages *vis-à-vis* collective purchasing of stocks from suppliers.[6] For over twenty years he made no attempt to unite their independent stores with his own. But in effect he expanded his influence and power more swiftly than he might have, had he attempted to raise all the necessary capital for new locations on his own.

CHARLTON AND KNOX

Earle Charlton formed his partnership with Seymour Knox (1861–1915) on 13 December 1889, and as such became the first member of the association not related either by blood or original Woolworth service. He was a full eleven years younger than Frank, and nine younger than Charles and most of the other partners, save Seymour Knox, only two years his senior. Knox already possessed two other stores of his own, plus some in association with others, including the Woolworths, and Earle's partnership with Knox could only have been possible because in his position as traveling salesman for Newell he had lived frugally and saved enough venture capital to enter fifty-fifty in starting a new store in

---

[6] Seymour Knox began in the family business in Hart, Michigan, then worked in a haberdashery in Grand Ledge, Mich., before accepting an invitation from cousin Frank Woolworth to open a five-and–ten at Reading, Penn. Each invested $1000, of which Knox borrowed $400 from Frank. This was around 1883. It flourished, but in 1886 Knox sold his share to another in order to finance his share with Frank in two larger stores, one at Newark, N.J., and another at Erie, Penn. The Newark store failed, but the Erie one succeeded. Some three years later Frank Woolworth sold his share of the Erie store and another of a store at Buffalo, N.Y., to Knox, principally in order to finance new stores of his own. It was from this base that Knox entered into his partnership with Charlton in Fall River.

tandem with Woolworth's cousin under a three-year agreement. The initial location was Fall River, Mass., and it was portentous because that city in the southeastern quadrant of the state became the Charlton homestead and administrative center of what turned into his considerable network of stores stretching from Fall River to the Maritime Provinces of Canada, and thence westward across both countries to their west coasts.

The first Knox & Charlton store opened in Fall River on 22 February 1890. It was agreed by both partners that Charlton would manage the store, with complete control over its operation and merchandising. Knox had become a close friend, and thus remained content to provide financial assistance to the partnership while overseeing his own stores in the Buffalo area. During the opening of the first store in Fall River, Charlton's wife Ida assisted in its operation and acted as its first cashier. The store became such an instantaneous success that Charlton, who had invested $100 in merchandise to stock it on its opening day, found his shelves bare by closing time. He was obliged to suspend operations the following day while he frantically re-stocked it, this time with $200 worth of goods. Then he quickly sold out again.

Fig. 2. The original Knox and Charlton 5 & 10 cent store which opened on February 22, 1890 on South Main Street in Fall River.

In all, his partnership with Knox lasted six years, during which they mutually operated four stores, and it is indicative of the complete trust that prevailed between the pair that on New Year's Day, 1893 they extended their association for three years on the stationery of the Broadway Hotel at Broadway and Twenty-Ninth Street, with not even a notary or witness to legalize it. (See Documentary Appendix, 1.) One can infer from this that there must have prevailed such an atmosphere of mutual trust among them—and possibly among most businessmen of the era—that there was no fear of the lawsuits and cheating so prevalent a century later. Especially the partners seemingly felt no need of documents drawn up by lawyers.[7]

THE PARTNERSHIP ENDS

The Charlton-Knox partnership terminated on New Year's Day, 1896. What prompted its dissolution—or, for that matter, that of any similar ones among five-and-ten partners—is mostly a matter of speculation. Knox and Charlton remained lifelong friends (and of course after 1912 became senior executives in the F. W. Woolworth Corporation), but it is obvious that at such a formative stage of the chain-retailing business, partnerships were constantly, even casually, being formed and dissolved as their principals' visions diverged. In the absence of company minutes or personal correspondence on the subject, one can only guess in the case of Knox and Charlton that when one of the partners could not convince the other that his new perception was appropriate to the investment of the other's capital, their partnership was fairly amicably dissolved.

This must have been especially so because the partners resided and managed parts of their common business in different cities. Consequently, in hours spent apart or in consultation with members of their separate staffs, they developed different ideas about where and how their enterprise should expand. It should be noted, however, that the differences seldom involved the *modus operandi* of any of the stores in themselves, and it is very likely that all those influenced by the

---

[7] This was hardly the case historically in other places and times. One might be tempted to speculate that in the formative stage of the American business structure much time and money was saved through the business ethic of mutual trust (and probably similarity of backgrounds in which church attendance and Christian ethic predominated).

experience of Frank Woolworth in merchandising followed closely his display and pricing ideas as well as his mixture of household notions, candies, perfumes, sheet music, and the like, and even coordinated their purchases in order to achieve the lowest possible prices. Where they must have differed was in regard to where and when to expand, and how much capital was needed.

FORMATION OF THE E. P. CHARLTON & CO. FIVE & TENS

The division of properties between the former partners left the Fall River, Hartford, and New Britain, Conn., stores in Charlton's hands, and deeded the one in Lowell, Mass., to Knox. Thereafter, in 1896, both partners went their own way, with Charlton forming his own company, and both beginning the rapid creation of new stores in their own selected regions. Knox expanded principally through the Midwest, and possessed nineteen stores by 1900, while Charlton initially opened nine stores in New England before he saw the greater opportunity in Canada and the regions of both countries west of the Rocky Mountains. Of the former partners, Knox expanded more rapidly as a consequence—at least in terms of numbers of new stores—while Charlton did not find his true style until 1 January 1899, when he sold off nine of his established stores to Frank Woolworth and gained enough capital for his projected western expansion.[8] Thereafter he, too, opened stores at breathtaking speed; by the time of his merger with Frank Woolworth and the other cousins in 1911–12, he had 53 stores, while Knox had 111.

Knox owed his more rapid expansion to the purchase of existing chains at the time of his incorporation, namely Seibert, Good & Co. and Foster, Post & Co., and nine stores from H. G. Woolworth & Co., bringing him to an immediate total of 35. Earle Charlton started all his own stores from the ground up. It would have been far easier—but consequently much more expensive—simply to have purchased established stores as Knox did. This was because Charlton had to identify the suitable candidate cities, find the ideal location, make the leases,

---

[8] He sold those at Hartford, Conn., Brockton, Mass., Meriden, Conn., Gloucester and New Bedford, Mass., Danbury, Conn., Lewiston, Me., Fitchburg and Lawrence, Mass. Of his stores prior to that date, Charlton kept only the original one at Fall River and another at New Britain, Conn.

redecorate and/or buy equipment. Finally, he had to bring in a team of experienced "starter" personnel, hire and train permanent staffs, and order and stock the merchandise. Knox, on the other hand, had to raise much more capital to buy ongoing stores, and of course he had to convert the already extant stores to his own organizational system, though this would not have been hard.

On 14 June 1907, E. P. Charlton & Co. was incorporated under the laws of the State of Connecticut with an authorized issue and outstanding capital stock of $2,000,000, divided into 20,000 shares of the par value of $100 each, of which $1,000,000 was 7% cumulative preferred stock and $1,000,000 was common stock. Charlton had incorporated at only $2,000,000, while Knox did so at exactly twice that much. But by 1910 the E. P. Charlton & Co. enjoyed the same profit margin (9.15% vs. 9%) with all of his stock privately owned, while Knox's profit had to be divided among the previous chain store owners that he had bought out. Charlton was thus rewarded for having kept his assets in his own hands.

The new corporation had its executive office in the Charlton Building in Fall River. E. P. Charlton & Co. Limited operated the company's units located in the Dominion of Canada.

Officers of the company were:

        Earle Perry Charlton – President
        E. A. Bardol – Vice President
        O. F. Douglas, Jr. – Secretary
        V. F. Thomas – Treasurer
        Miss I. H. Morrison – Assistant Treasurer

Whether is was coincidence or merely as a result of the close cooperation between the Woolworth "family" of five-and-ten owners, it became apparent upon their mega-merger in 1912 that none of the participants' stores occupied the same territory or competed with one another. It could well be that Seymour Knox and Charlton—not to speak of Frank Woolworth—settled upon their future territories and strategies even before they parted company. The reasoning behind Charlton's selling of his nine northeastern stores to Woolworth in 1899 surely must have been known to him and the others, that Charlton had staked out his own unique new territory for expansion in Canada, along the northern tier of states and westward to the Pacific.

Fig. 3. Earle P. Charlton

The situation in Canada on the eve of Charlton's expansion to the north is difficult to ascertain. It is very possible that the five-and-ten mania among imitators and competitors, as created by the success of Frank Woolworth, had not gone nearly as quickly in Canada, if because there was less capital available there and the business climate was less innovative. Hence, it may have seemed to one as perceptive as Charlton that he would run little risk in introducing his five-and-tens to virtually any Canadian city of appropriate size and any American one distant enough from the trends of the Northeast and Midwest. He certainly behaved as though this were his conviction: he expanded at an exhausting pace between 1899 and 1911, at ten entirely new stores of his own making per annum.

CHARLTON REACHES UP TO CANADA AND OUT TO THE WEST COAST

The dates and sequence of the openings of E. P. Charlton & Co. stores after 1899 can be traced through existent letterhead stationery used by Charlton for his correspondence. Every time he opened a new store, he would add the store to his descriptive letterhead. This would necessitate the purchase of new stationery after each new store was opened.

It will be remembered that the only stores Earle Charlton retained after his sale of nine stores to F. W. Woolworth in 1899 was the original one in Fall River on South Main Street, and another store in New Britain. At a later date, he would open a second store in Fall River on Pleasant Street.

In looking for a place to expand his young company, Charlton checked out the locations of friendly competitors and determined that their stores were mostly all located in New England and the northeastern coast. Frank Woolworth and his brother Charles had New York-based companies, Knox's stores were concentrated in the upper New York area, and Fred Kirby had a Pennsylvania-based company that ventured to the south. With all of New England and the northeast potentially covered by his friendly business associates, Charlton looked north to Canada for the expansion of his fledgling 5 & 10 cent company.

Charlton's company became international when his first store opened in Montreal in 1900, followed by a second store in Montreal and subsequent stores in Ottawa, Quebec, St. John and Halifax in New

Brunswick, a third store in Montreal and his first store in Nova Scotia, in Amherst. He was now ready to venture into new territory.

In early 1905, Charlton opened his first store on the West Coast, giving his chain of stores an intercontinental flavor. His initial West Coast store was located on Washington Street, in Portland, Oregon. The store was an instant success, and it encouraged him to push on to California, where he felt the real potential lay for bigger and more profitable stores.

His first venture into California was in downtown Los Angeles where he opened his largest store on South Broadway in late 1905. As it turned out, the Los Angeles and Portland stores became the highest sales volume stores in the Charlton chain, followed by his original store in Fall River.

The Los Angeles store opening was followed by additional California stores in Stockton, Sacramento, San Jose, and Fresno. He then turned north to open a store in Tacoma, Wash., and one in Sherbrooke, Quebec.

Fig. 4. On February 29, 1908, in celebration of E. P. Charlton's 18th anniversary, this congratulatory piece appeared in the Fall River *Globe*.

In early 1906 Charlton opened another large store in downtown San Francisco. He had just left the city and returned home to Fall River when, on 18 April 1906, he received a telegram announcing the store had been totally destroyed. The great San Francisco earthquake had struck the city at 5:13 in the morning and, along with the great fire that followed, the city was in ruins. Within an hour after receiving the telegram, Charlton gave instructions to rebuild the store, and within thirty days a new store was built on a newly acquired location, and it was the first retail business to reopen in San Francisco after the earthquake and fire.

After San Francisco, Charlton established two stores in the state of Washington, at Tacoma and Spokane, his second store in San Francisco, on Mission Street, and another across the San Francisco Bay, on Broadway in Oakland.

Moving on, Charlton went south to open additional new California stores in San Diego, Pasadena, Riverside, San Bernardino, and Long Beach, and a second store in Los Angeles. It was at this time that he opened another store in the northwest, in Seattle. Meanwhile, he remained active in Canada, opening new stores at Sherbrooke, Quebec, and Winnipeg, Manitoba. All of these stores were operational by the end of 1908.

By April of 1909, Charlton had ventured into the Rocky Mountain area to open stores in Butte, Mont., and Ogden and Salt Lake City, Utah. (Anyone who has traveled to Butte, even now, can visualize how difficult it must have been to start up a store in such an isolated and out-of-the-way section of the country, from a base in Fall River, Mass.) Next came stores in Walla Walla and Bellingham, Washington, and Vancouver, British Columbia.

A year later, in 1910, he had added two new Canadian stores, at Moncton, New Brunswick, and at Victoria, British Columbia. The Victoria store inherited the store number of no. 32, Long Beach, which had been closed. Then, surprisingly, Charlton returned nearer home, to Connecticut, where he created three new stores at Norwich, Bristol, and New London. And by the summer of 1911 he had opened stores at scattered sites across the two neighboring countries: new stores in Salem, Ore., Aberdeen and Everett, Wash., Boise, Idaho, and the rest in Canada at Brockville and Fort William, Ontario, at Sydney, Nova Scotia, and St. Hyacinthe and St. Johns, Quebec.

It was also at this time that Charlton opened his third store in San Francisco, located on Market Street in close proximity to his first store, which was destroyed by the earthquake of 1906. This store would become his flagship store on the West Coast, and one of his highest volume stores.[9]

In 1911, the final two E. P. Charlton stores were added: in Missoula, Montana, and Bakersfield, California, bringing his grand total to fifty-three stores. These were all merged into the new Woolworth Co. on 1 January 1912.

Listed on the following pages are the ten top E. P. Charlton & Co. stores in sales volume for the year 1911, and the fifty-three stores that Charlton opened, from his first store in Fall River in 1890 to his last store in Bakersfield, California, in late 1911:

THE TOP TEN CHARLTON STORES IN 1911 BEFORE THE MERGER

Stores	Sales
1. Los Angeles, Cal. (store no. 14), 431 S. Broadway	$372,126
2. Portland, Ore. (store no. 41), 288–90 Washington St.	$227,760
3. Fall River, Mass. (store no. 44), 91 S. Main St.	$215,184
4. Salt Lake City, Utah (store no. 61), 251–53 S. Main St.	$178,711
5. San Francisco, Cal. (store no. 64), 891 Market St.	$174,915
6. Montreal, Que. (store no. 76), 356 St. Lawrence St.	$151,114
7. Montreal, Que. (store no. 85), 395 St. Catherine W.	$144,324
8. Seattle, Wash. (store no. 96), 1305 2nd Ave.	$136,083
9. Vancouver, B.C. (store no. 101), 339 Hastings St., W.	$132,448
10. Tacoma, Wash. (store no. 105), 1108 Pacific Ave.	$129,460

[9] When store no. 64 was moved across Market Street (to Powell and Market) in 1954, it became the largest store in sales volume in the Woolworth Co. Earle Perry Charlton's grandson E. P. Charlton II was assistant manager of that store in that year.

E. P. Charlton Stores at the Time of the Merger with the F. W. Woolworth Company, 1 January 1912

Store	City	Address
1.	Fall River, Mass.	91–103 S. Main St.
2.	New Brunswick, Ct.	218–220 Main St.
3.	Fall River, Mass.	1353 & 1359 Pleasant St.
4.	Montreal, Que.	395 Catherine, West
5.	Montreal, Que.	356 St. Lawrence St.
6.	Ottawa, Ont.	172–176 Sparks St.
7.	Quebec, Que.	149–151 St. Joseph St.
8.	St. John, N.B.	93–97 King St.
9.	Halifax, N.S.	79–81 Barrington St.
10.	Montreal, Que.	489 St. Catherine, East
11.	Amherst, N.S.	155 Victoria St.
12.	Portland, Ore.	288–290 Washington St.
13.	Los Angeles, Cal.	431–435 South Broadway
14.	Stockton, Cal.	422–426 E. Main St.
15.	Sacramento, Cal.	522–524 K St.
16.	San Jose, Cal.	29 S. First St.
17.	Fresno, Cal.	932 J St.
18.	Tacoma, Wash.	1108 Pacific Ave.
19.	Sherbrooke, Que.	145 Wellington St.
20.	San Francisco, Cal.	1347 Fillmore
21.	Oakland, Cal.	1008 Broadway
22.	San Francisco, Cal.	2554 Mission St.
23.	Seattle, Wash.	1305 2nd Ave.
24.	San Diego, Cal.	840 Fifth St.
25.	Butte, Mont.	118–120 Main St.
26.	Riverside, Cal.	835 Main St.
27.	Pasadena, Cal.	95 E. Colorado St.
28.	Ogden, Utah	2363 Washington Ave.
29.	Spokane, Wash.	809 Riverside Ave.
30.	San Bernardino, Cal.	518–520 Third St.
31.	Los Angeles, Cal.	113–115 N. Spring St.

Continued on next page.

Continued from previous page.

Store	City	Address
32.	Victoria, B.C.[10]	1110 Government St.
33.	Winnipeg, Man.	304 Portage Ave.
34.	Walla Walla, Wash.	17 W. Main St.
35.	Vancouver, B.C.	339 Hastings St. West
36.	Bellingham, Wash.	120–126 W. Holly St.
37.	Salt Lake City, Utah	251–253 S. Main St.
38.	New London, Ct.	80–82 State St.
39.	Norwich, Ct.	157–159 Main St.
40.	Bristol, Ct.	148 Main St.
41.	Moncton, B.C.	689–695 Main St.
42.	San Francisco, Cal.	891–893 Market St.
43.	Salem, Ore.	State St.
44.	Aberdeen, Wash.	208 E. Heron St.
45.	Brockville, Ont.	65 King St.
46.	Everett, Wash.	1818–20 Hewitt Ave.
47.	Fort William, Ont.	423 Victoria Ave.
48.	Boise, Idaho	915 Main St.
49.	Sydney, N.S.	Charlotte St.
50.	St. Hyacinthe, Que.	128 Cascade St.
51.	St. Johns, Que.	86–88 Richelieu St.
52.	Missoula, Mont.	217 N. Higgins Avenue
53.	Bakersfield, Cal.	1408 Nineteenth St.

[10] Store no. 32 was originally assigned to Long Beach, Cal., but the store number was re–assigned to Victoria, B.C., after the Long Beach store was closed.

II

THE KAPSTEIN WINDOW

WHAT ONE CAN DO WITH A TYPEWRITER, carbon copies, and postage stamps from a great distance was proven again and again by Earle Charlton from his office at 93–101 South Main Street in Fall River. It might seem impossible in an age of computers, conference calls, and e-mail to carry out expansions and keep track of fifty-three stores, many of them on the Pacific coast of the United States and Canada, but this is exactly what he did.

Virtually all administrative material from the E. P. Charlton Co. has been lost in the course of time, something highly usual in the case of defunct companies, especially in days before information technology, even microfilming, existed; the filing cases simply took up too much room and somewhere along the line the decision was made to destroy their contents. All that exists today to suggest how Charlton operated his business is a fragmentary survival of seventy-eight original letters dating between 1908 to 1912,[1] and (with one exception) all written to or by Charlton's chief inspector, the invaluable and energetic Simon Kapstein, who was entrusted with the role of troubleshooter and occasionally store opener, and traveled constantly on the west coast. In fact, it was during precisely these five years that most of the new stores in that region were inaugurated. Several opened in the two-year period prior to the merger with Woolworth, and it is obvious that these footholds on the Pacific coast were the most valuable to Charlton because they represented a prime network in an area which Frank Woolworth greatly desired. In fact, it was undoubtedly these Western and Pacific stores that allowed Charlton to strike such a favorable arrangement with Woolworth in 1911,

---

[1] Forty-four of these letters are transcribed in the Documentary Appendix at the end of this book. Two of these letters have been included in the illustrations.

one which virtually allowed him to do as he pleased for the remainder of his life.

CHARLTON'S LETTERS TO SIMON KAPSTEIN

One gathers that the letters had first been preserved by Kapstein himself, and then turned over to the Woolworth Co. after the great merger. In this irreplaceable collection, nearly all the letters were written by Charlton to Kapstein, providing instructions on how to go about his tasks and offering personal advice.[2] Because pages are often lacking and other, missing letters and events are alluded to in the surviving ones, it is obvious that the cache is not complete, and that many documents were lost, most likely through carelessness in the course of time.

Before examining the letters and what they reveal, it is worthwhile to tell something of his trusted employee, Simon Kapstein, who, as a young associate, so faithfully served Charlton first on the east coast, in Canada, and finally in the development of his west coast stores. Kapstein was born in Fall River in 1886; during a warm summer day in 1902 he graduated from high school. He writes, "during an early summer warm spell, after listening to the inspiring platitudes of the principal, Mr. Benson, a former Civil War captain, I walked downtown to Main Street, stopping to look into shop windows and looking into stores." He continued:

> Fall River was a town of small, individually owned businesses better known as "mama-papa" operations. Main Street in our town, as in so many towns of our country, was just what its name implied, the center of the local business world. That is where I wanted to be. No more newspaper routes for me—that was a job for a schoolboy and I needed to find a man's work that would lead to a real career. As I plodded up one side of the street and down the other, looking for the elusive "Help Wanted" sign propped in a window corner, knowing that the hand-lettered signs that read "Boy Wanted for Summer Work" were no longer directed at me, my eye was caught by a brilliant, red-and-gold sign glittering in

---

[2] The surviving letters were discovered in a Woolworth file at the regional office in Burlingame, Cal., by Earle Perry Charlton II, the founder's grandson and co-author of this book, during his tenure as regional manager of F. W. Woolworth's thirteen-state Pacific region. The West Coast regional office had been moved from downtown San Francisco to Burlingame in the 1950s.

the hot afternoon sunlight. I'd always liked that sign. It read simply, E. P. CHARLTON COMPANY 5 & 10 CENT STORE.

I liked the idea of incorporating the prices in the vivid sign. It implied a kind of honesty and a straightforward approach that appealed to me, and besides, I thought that the windows crammed with bright, new merchandise were marvelous. It was a wonderful thing to be able to offer quantities of such varied merchandise to all the people at low prices which almost everybody could afford. There were a good number of children staring, fascinated, at a big display of toys. I joined them, admiring the windows and was just as fascinated as the children. Before I knew it, I was in the store, really looking for the first time, at the arrangement of toy and candy counters, at jewelry, and at hardware. The next morning, with my mother and father at the breakfast table, my father spoke up and said, "Well, my son, what do you intend to do with yourself?" I said I didn't know yet, but that I'd surely find a good job somewhere and that I planned to look immediately. As I walked on Main Street, I realized that Mr. Charlton was an important man. His store was the main office of a small, but rapidly growing chain of 5 & 10 stores in the eastern part of the United States and Canada. Did I dare? I took a deep breath and approached a dignified man standing just inside the door.... He obviously had something to do with the store, so I asked him if I could please meet Mr. Charlton. He said, "I am Mr. Charlton." I introduced myself and told him I was looking for a job that would continue after the vacation time, and, please, could I get some work in his store? He asked me a lot of questions about what I intended to do and why. At last he told me that he would give me a job in the stock room, and on Monday morning of the following week, I went to work as a stock boy.[3]

Simon's pay, as he reported, was a disappointing $3 a week or 50¢ per day. But he persevered, and even enrolled in a local business school for a two-year evening course in management, as he said, surrounding himself with business periodicals pertaining to stock and floor work and merchandising. From then on promotions and raises followed, first as assistant to the receiving clerk, then to the clerk's job when that man received a promotion to store manager. There followed a variety of jobs in various aspects of company operations, including window-trimming. He received his first reprimand from Charlton when reporting for work an hour late after trimming windows late into the night. That was no excuse, said his master, "No matter how late you work you are to be here at 8 o'clock in the morning." Later, Kapstein wrote, Mr. Charlton

---

[3] Simon Kapstein's remarks are taken from an unpublished autobiography he wrote in his last years, which was made available to E. P. Charlton II by Kapstein's son, Robert A. Kerner, of San Francisco, and reproduced here with his permission.

apologized. This would confirm that Charlton was a stern, but fair employer.

GO WEST, YOUNG MAN

After he had been with the company for three-and-one-half years, Charlton approached him with the words "Simon, our store in San Francisco has been entirely destroyed by the earthquake and fire." He asked Kapstein if he would like to go west to help re-establish the store in San Francisco, and suggested he discuss it with his parents. It was decided that at twenty, he was too young. A year later, he was offered another opportunity, this time to help open several new stores in Canada, which he accepted and did for a year-and-a-half. Finally, in 1908, Charlton dispatched him to investigate the possibilities of establishing new outlets in Ogden, Reno, and Spokane. From then on, as the letters demonstrate, he became Charlton's right-hand man on the West Coast, sometimes opening and managing new stores, sometimes trouble-shooting, and always on the move.

But let us return to the letters and their contents. That the documents were in Kapstein's possession, and not copies of letters to him retained in Fall River, is indicated by the original typing on letterhead stationery, often signed in Charlton's own hand. Moreover, there are fold marks on all the ones emanating from his Fall River office, showing that they were inserted into envelopes, while the occasional reply by Kapstein to his employer is on plain paper, unsigned, unfolded and in fuzzy carbon impression, indicating that it was a copy he retained for his own records. All this having been said, the glimpse the papers afford into the workings of the company and its proprietor is unique and invaluable because it provides the only window extant on the workings of the E. P. Charlton Co. and the thoughts of its founder during the years he was building his empire.[4]

---

[4] In all commercial enterprises, preservation of such records is hardly the norm. After a certain number of years, papers were routinely destroyed (obviously the interests of future historians were not considered, while conservation of space was). It would be remarkable if more than one or two percent of documentation from the nineteenth or early twentieth centuries has survived, much less from earlier times.

Charlton seemingly did not attempt to correspond personally and directly with his store managers, but rather kept a constant vigil on their figures and inventories and then addressed Kapstein in regard to what measures should be taken to remedy the problems that arose. Although Kapstein was Earle Charlton's favorite troubleshooter on the west coast, he was also the company's number-two man there, sharing responsibilities with Harry P. Hermance, at once manager of Charlton's San Francisco store and his district manager. Charlton, who felt great affection for the young man, would often start his letters to Kapstein with "My dear Simon."

Above all else, the letters serve as testimonials to Charlton's qualities of mind that made him a millionaire in the first place: his precision, his tolerance, and his uncanny ability to diagnose problems and orchestrate his growing retail empire from afar. They reveal that his success was no fluke because they reflect his enormous grasp of affairs in his company, not to mention his capacity and drive. It is also obvious from Kapstein's earnestness and capacity for work that Charlton was successful because he knew how to judge and trust the men who were his eyes and ears.

By 1908, there were thirty-three stores, stretching from the mother establishment downstairs on South Main Street in Fall River to San Francisco, including nine in Canada. As noted previously, there is no documentation covering exactly what ideas prompted Charlton to range so far afield after establishing his first three stores close to home (two in Fall River itself and one in New Britain, Conn.), but his decision to do so certainly had much to do with his perception that locations in the northeast were rapidly being covered by the stores of his friendly competitors the two Woolworths, Knox, and Kirby, who would be quick enough to develop outlets there.

From establishment of his new outlets in eastern Canada, Charlton vaulted across North America, and opened his first American west-coast store in Portland, Oregon, before opening his initial store in California, in downtown Los Angeles. Four more California stores followed before returning to the northwest to open a store in Tacoma, Washington.

Meanwhile, as hundreds of letters, reports and papers must have poured into Charlton's Fall River offices daily with details of sales, orders, and payments, he knew that the West-Coast economy was developing at a fast clip and offered enormous opportunity to chain retailers. By 1912, the year of his merger with F. W. Woolworth, Charlton ruled over fifty-three stores, the majority of them in the west.

THE TROUBLESHOOTER

Even though Kapstein was only the number-two man on the west coast, it would appear from the letters that he did supervise in the actual openings of new stores throughout the region. His main job, however, seems to have been as a troubleshooter, who traveled from store to store "putting out fires" and helping the managers when things did not go smoothly. He was instructed to travel to a location and stay with it (as in a letter of 1908 regarding the new Spokane store) until it operated smoothly, and to remedy any errors in personnel and procedure that were likely to occur when new branches were constantly being opened and in rapid succession. No information exists on how managers were chosen in the first instance, but some seem to have been trained in the east, while others were developed on the spot, some probably as managers or founders of independent stores. It is barely possible (though no evidence for such exists) that Charlton's agents simply purchased individual variety stores already in existence, thereupon expanding them and making them over. Kapstein was generally called in when sales of a given store were flagging, especially in proportion to the size of the town in which it was located, or else dishonesty was suspected, or the manager was floundering, distracted, or incompetent.

Back in Fall River, Charlton continually checked the latest Bradstreet reports on the economic health of the municipality, and he took pains to make sure that the manager had adequate stocks and knew how to move them, if necessary, through timely price reductions. Moreover, he kept track of every manager and assistant and was at pains to understand and accommodate their needs. In San Francisco, for example, he worried that Mr. Hermance had too many other irons in the fire and was neglecting his store; he counseled Kapstein to give him assistance and, if possible, straighten him out.[5] To cite another instance, he believed a certain Mr. Upton in Vancouver to be a very good manager, but the man had professed himself to be unhappy there and wanted to leave for southern California, claiming he could not stand the

---

[5] Letter of 26 May 1910; see Documentary Appendix, 12.

weather in Canada. Charlton advised Kapstein that the real trouble was Upton's wife, who longed to return to her home. (Vancouver actually possessed a very healthful climate, he averred.) But, he said that he wished to retain Upton and keep him happy, and would comply with his request for a store in southern California as soon as a suitable opening should occur.[6]

But when it turned out that Upton had suddenly resigned, as had come to Charlton's ears because Kapstein had been abrupt with him, Charlton advised:

> Now, Simon, let this be a lesson to you in the future. You have a certain amount of authority and supervision, but never show it on entering a store with a manager, or in taking the place of one removed. Go about this work diplomatically, making the manager feel that you came to assist him; that you are dependent, somewhat, upon his advice in local matters; that you want his assistance, and make the manager feel when you are in the capacity of inspector that you came only to assist him and suggest.

> Some managers are very set in their ways—and they take offense at a man coming in and pulling their stock to pieces and saying, "Here, this is not right, that is not right." You may not know the conditions of the town. The way to go about it is to state that Los Angeles, or Seattle, or Tacoma have been following out this or that method of showing goods and have made a big success of it, and instruct the girls and the managers how you would like the work done.

> In this way, you can get good results all around, whereas on the other hand, you will antagonize the manager, and the moment you are out, doubtless put the goods back as they were before. If you can show him conclusively that it is profitable to do as you suggest, then there will be benefit all around.[7]

In response to Kapstein's own expressed desire for a position back in Fall River, he took an almost paternal tone:

> I can give you no encouragement this present year of being able to place you in a permanent location, I do not see the opening for you to make any such amount of money or to be of any such assistance to us as you are in the capacity of inspector. I trust that Mr. Bardol has talked this matter over with you. I want you to realize that we appreciate your services and have the greatest interest in your future and your welfare. In an organization of this kind, there must be experts in every department. These changes will come in good time

---

[6] Letter of 15 April 1909; see Documentary Appendix, 7.
[7] Letter of 26 May 1909; see Documentary Appendix, 9.

and I want you to allow me to be the judge of when and where to place you. [The] enclosed check balances your account for the year 1910, as per vote by the Board of Directors, Jan. 1st. I trust, my boy, that you are putting your money in safe investments and not in any "wild-cat" schemes.[8]

SEXUAL HARRASSMENT

Sexual harassment had not become a national issue in 1911, but even then the Charlton Co. would tolerate little of it. On April 7, Kapstein received a telegram followed by a letter from E. A. Bardol, Charlton's vice president, that their bank in Butte, Montana, had telegraphed him that the manager of their store there, a Mr. Sprungman, had been absent from it for several days—as the assistant manager, a Mr. Williams, then explained, in order to sober up from heavy drinking bouts. Kapstein was ordered to take the first train for Montana and investigate, and he wasted no time, arriving there only four days later. In a letter to Earle Charlton, dated April 13, he wrote:

> I trust you will agree with me that in letting Mr. Sprungman go, as I did, was to the best interests of the Company, and protects us from some cheap "John Lawyer." We have here a force of help to be proud of, all are ladylike, courteous, and clean-cut. It would not be to our advantage to make any changes in the help. After thinking [it] over, it would not be doing the young lady justice who refused to tie up with Mr. Sprungman; I further gave her credit for doing so. She is a clean-cut little girl, honest and of a nice family, and Mr. Sprungman was trying to take advantage of her. After going into several confidential chats with the clerks of the store, I find that Mr. Sprungman has tried to propose to several of the young ladies. If Mr. Sprungman was that weak to allow drink to upset him over a girl, I am sure you or anyone else has no further use for him.[9]

CIRCUMSPECTION

Charlton was pleased with Kapstein's handling of the situation in Butte, but he soon ordered him back to Spokane, where the store there had been sadly underperforming. Although it was Kapstein's job as inspector to

---

[8] Letter of 28 January 1911; see Documentary Appendix, 21.
[9] Letter or 13 April 1911; see Documentary Appendix, 25.

bring stability to stagnating locations, it is illuminating of Charlton's meticulous attention to detail that he took the time personally to instruct his protégé in exactly the course he wished him to follow. He explained the matter thus:

> There is something very, very wrong, and I believe it is wholly with the management. This store should do on an average of $800 to $1,000 and on Saturdays, $1,200 to $1,500 easily. Now it is up to you to make the showing of your life, by going in as assistant manager and I shall dictate policy to Mr. Baldwin, whereby your recommendations will be carried out until proved.
>
> I do not believe the man is paying attention to business. I do not think the windows are snappy. I should cover them with strip posters. Put attractive specials in the window and watch the floor like a cat does a mouse [especially] the sales slips from each register. The first thing, when you go in there, get up a schedule book [for] yourself privately and take down every register. Read these carefully yourself on Sunday and see how they compare. Have slips for every clerk and relieve those who are not doing business. Get a basis and then start clerks in, the best regulars, on a bonus of 2% on additional sales over the amounts they have averaged for three weeks after cleaning out unnecessary help, getting their salaries down to a basis of not more than 7%. This is your first work. The help['s] figures would be all right, if they were doing a business of $6,000 a week.
>
> After you have thoroughly studied the situation, give me your ideas. I believe that with proper management in four weeks' time, the business can be doubled.... My plan for you is, if you are all tired out, go into the Yellowstone to some nice little hotel and spend a week after leaving Spokane. As far as chasing around the country for a vacation is concerned, there is no rest in it and it will do you no good.[10]

This passage, one among many in his correspondence with Kapstein, illustrates his infinite capacity for attention, and, specifically, attention to detail. It is also obvious that while he was exacting, he was very loyal to his subordinates and was as careful to further their well-being. Even though he denied Kapstein's wish to return to the east because he could not dispense with his valuable services in the Pacific region, he also promised Kapstein liberal bonuses—including an extra $1000 if he succeeded in turning the Spokane store around.

---

[10] Letter of 14 June 1911; see Documentary Appendix, 29.

Fig. 5. The E. P. Charlton 5 & 10 cent store on Washington Street in Portland, Ore., (1905) was the first of Charlton's West Coast stores.

Fig. 6. Interior of the Portland, Oregon, store. Note the wooden floors and the imprinted "tin" ceiling.

One would gather from the correspondence that the least of Charlton's worries involved display, stocking, and accounting procedures—for these all depended upon subordinate personnel—and one gathers that finding and keeping reliable and conscientious managers was his biggest headache. The same names crop up again and again in the letters—Hermance, Files, Baldwin, Ohiser, Sprungman, Upton, and the Williamses, and the difficulties they presented to Fall River comprise a litany of foibles that continue to haunt businesses to this day. Files in Spokane had poor control over his inventory and ordered goods already in stock, Baldwin was suspected of dishonesty or incompetence, Ohiser withdrew unauthorized cash from the till, Sprungman in Butte had problems with the opposite sex and drink, Upton (or his spouse) longed to escape from Vancouver, the elder Williams in Seattle was old and too frequently sick to run his store adequately, while Hermance in San Francisco had too many outside interests and was spotted by absenteeism. Then Williams the younger, who succeeded Sprungman in Butte, got himself into trouble, jail, and lawsuits, apparently because he attempted too many business deals on the side with too little capital.

HUMANE HANDLING

Problems with the younger Williams in Butte in fact afford some interesting insights, if not into Williams's difficulties, which remain murky in the letters, but into Charlton's tolerance and desire to give his employees the benefit of every doubt, and into the honesty of Simon Kapstein. The younger Williams, it will be remembered, was given management of the store when Sprungman was discharged, and he began with good references and fair auguries. But then disturbing reports began to arrive in Fall River. On 15 May 1911, Charlton wrote Kapstein:

> We have received a long letter from the cashier of the Butte store, who has made statements that this Williams, who is now store manager, is a liar and many other things, that he has taken letters addressed to you out of the waste basket and pieced them together to see their purport, and that he has shown the wife nothing of [her] cashier['s job] and of the business and that she knows nothing. Now I imagine that a great deal of this is talk, and it may be a good plan that she has been eliminated, but I have never thoroughly made up my mind that a man is perfectly conscientious and honest who undermines another for the sake of securing the position and this is apparently what Williams did in

both telegrams and letters. It begins to look to me as though he were a very sly boy. He may be all fight, and I hope he is, but your trouble in my opinion is that you take too much stock in what these men tell you, that they pat you on the back and make you believe anything.[11]

Next, things became worse. On September 27th Charlton wrote Kapstein in Missoula, where a new Charlton store was opening:

As soon as this store can be conveniently left, say Tuesday or Wednesday, and if Gardner is competent to manage it, you must go down to Butte and stay there until further notice, and thoroughly investigate this Williams' episode. He has been extradited, and is now in jail in Portland under $1500.00 cash bonds. If worthy of assistance, we wish to help him in any reasonable way we can, but if it looks as if the other side had a good story, and all that he has done is illegal, or else there is no justice in Montana. If he has done the thing as alleged, he is a natural-born crook and we do not want him in our business. I feel very sorry for his wife, and if she is still in the Butte store and doing well, we want to assist her by allowing her to remain there.

However, it would be a temptation for her or anyone else in the present case to handle any of our funds. It seems strange that Butte has had such a series of incompetent managers which have cost us money, and I should be delighted to see someone put in that store who could bring it up in the class that I know it should stand. Let me hear from you when you arrive there.[12]

Almost at the same time, in fact on September 26, Mrs. Williams wrote Kapstein:

Your letter was received this morning, and I was very glad to get it... . I was feeling blue, but your letter cheered me. Mr. Williams left yesterday afternoon at 3 o'clock. The sheriff [from Portland] played a mean trick, he said they would leave at 7 o'clock and that he could come to the store and get his suit case before he left; instead of doing that he sneaked him off at 3 o'clock. [He] wouldn't let him see me or get his suit case, so I sent it c/o Mr. Baldwin. Papa went down to the train, but couldn't find him; [the sheriff] must have hid him somewhere. [He] was afraid we were going to start something else to hold him here longer, [and] he was mad to think he had to stay as long as he did.

Mr. Noyes wrote to the [Masonic] lodge at Portland and told them to do all they could for him. The Butte lodge were back of him, and the telegram I got from Charlton Co. this morning shows that everything will be alright... . No one is here yet to take charge of the store, but [I] will try and keep things straight till

---

[11] Letter of 15 May 1911; see Documentary Appendix, 28.
[12] Letter of 27 September 1911; see Documentary Appendix, 36.

some one arrives. Will send your letter to Jack as soon as I find out where he is.[13]

By October 9th, the picture for Williams looked considerably brighter. On that date, Kapstein wrote Charlton:

I arrived in Butte at one o'clock Sunday [after]noon. Before seeing Williams I made arrangements to have an interview with the Master of the Masonic Lodge, and he told me all he knew of Williams' case. Also saw the Secretary of the same lodge, who told me a like story.

I afterwards made arrangements for an appointment with his attorney, and all seemed to agree that M. Seller & Co. had no case against Williams. Baxter County, Oregon, refused to indict Williams, they having given him a clear title in bankruptcy; but Multnomah County, in which Portland is located, and Mr. Sellers having a lot of influence there and Williams not being personally known there, issued the indictment. Therefore, upon presenting the requisition to the Lieut. Governor of Montana, he, the Lieutenant, through courtesy to the Governor of Oregon, signed the requisition.

The basis upon which Mr. Seller placed their case is that Williams neglected to put in three of his assets in filing his papers; one for $500, which he borrowed from his uncle, one for $200, which he borrowed from a friend of his; and $475, which he owed M. Seller & Co.

The attorney told me in spite of all this they had no legal ground on which to base their case, and that they intended to push the case to a finish and make M. Seller & Co. pay heavily for it.

Personally, I think that M. Seller & Co., after finding out that Williams was working for us and that he, being only a boy, they would take legal steps to scare him, and they wrote Williams several threatening letters; whereupon Williams, rather than obtain the notoriety, offered a settlement of $50 a month until the full amount was cleared up, which the boy never should have done.

M. Seller, on the other hand, when he received his letter, in my opinion, noticed that Williams was "taking water" and pressed him for the total amount in one payment, which of course Williams could never do, as he hadn't any money to do it with.
I personally feel now, after holding conversations with several of the gentlemen who were interested in the case, that M. Seller will eventually try to drop the case in order to protect himself. Personally, I lay all the confidence in the world in Williams and find both him and his wife to the work and trustworthy, and am

---

[13] Letter of 26 September 1911; see Documentary Appendix, 35.

quite sure that not a cent of our money has been touched. I furthermore think that no man, under local conditions, can run this store more economically [than] Williams does. The store looked pretty good, although the shelf trims are the same, in many instances, as those I put up in May. The stock room is pretty much piled up with imported and domestic goods, which had accumulated in Williams' absence. He still has a very heavy stock, and I will try to relieve him a little of it by shipping some down to the Missoula store.

Mrs. Williams, poor girl, is worked to the limit and is almost worn out. The boy is anxious to make good and feels for the interests of our Company, that the showing this store will make, will be equal to any ... in Butte. I gave him a good, stiff talking to before his wife and uncle, and somehow I take a liking to the boy and above all I would be greatly disappointed if he fails to make good. I hardly think it necessary for me to put in any great length of time here, as everything seems to be running smoothly and I will no doubt plan to return to Missoula not later than Thursday.[14]

On the following day, Kapstein wrote Charlton that Mr. Seller had dropped his case against the young manager.[15] Unfortunately, the story must end here, for the papers contain no further news. What lesson can be drawn from the case, however, is that Charlton stood solidly behind his employees and did not rush hastily to judgment—for after all, Mrs. Williams reported even before Kapstein's arrival on the scene that she had received a comforting telegram from Fall River. Many companies would certainly have discharged Williams willy-nilly once he had been arrested, but Charlton instead elected to give him the benefit of the doubt until Kapstein could investigate.

Mrs. Williams appears to have been a supportive wife who saved her husband's job, but she was not the only woman who could shoulder a man's responsibilities and perform them even better than he, in this case of Mr. Ohiser, the Salem manager. A year before, Earle Charlton wrote Simon Kapstein that although he had sent a Miss Lottie Kimball to work in the west principally for the sake of her health, she had proved her worth by blowing the whistle on Ohiser; it seems she had discovered his fingers in the cash register.[16] In the interim, she had taken over the store and was running it ably, pending her relief.

---

[14] Letter of 9 October 1911; see Documentary Appendix, 38.
[15] Letter of 10 October 1911; see Documentary Appendix, 39.
[16] Letter of 10 October 1910; see Documentary Appendix, 16.

END OF AN EPOCH

As for the relationship between Charlton and Kapstein, there is no final information because the correspondence ends abruptly on 8 February 1912, a full month after Charlton & Co. was merged with Woolworth. The last letter between Kapstein and the home office, dated 8 February 1912, deals with Kapstein's salary over 1911, written not by Charlton but by E. A. Bardol, his vice-president and brother-in-law. Bardol said:

> As you no doubt know, Mr. Charlton is ill, and unable to take up these various matters. Which he knows more about than does the writer. In any event, I have a check drawn for the difference between what you have withdrawn for the year and an amount equal to that received by you last year, which I believe will be in accord with Mr. Charlton's wishes. Should there be any change from this, after his convalescence, and he takes these matters in hand, you will hear from him further.
>
> In the meantime, we wish you the best of success under the new management.[17]

After the merger, there is no additional correspondence from Kapstein, at least as an employee of the E. P. Charlton Co. Bardol (who ultimately became a vice-president in the new F. W. Woolworth Co.) suggested that he would find a place in the new organization, and that things might continue for him much as before. That Charlton had the greatest regard for his inspector is demonstrated by a letter he had written him the preceding August 14th, one which seems to hint that even then a deal with Woolworth might have been pending:

> You have ... been a valuable asset and there will always be a good position for you as long as this firm exists or its successors, if there ever are any... .[18]

Charlton, in fact, required that all his employees must be re-employed by the Woolworth management. Such was certainly the case with Kapstein. But there was a sinister factor at play: intolerance within the Woolworth organization.

Simon Kapstein was Jewish, and the F. W. Woolworth Co. did not have any employees of the Jewish faith at senior supervisory levels.

---

[17] Letter of 8 February 1912; see Documentary Appendix, 42.
[18] Letter of 14 August 1911; see Documentary Appendix, 32.

Charlton did not discriminate, hiring his personnel for their work ethic and productivity, not by race or religion, and he insisted that Woolworth hire all of his employees at all levels. Kapstein persevered, and he became one of the few members of the Jewish faith in a supervisory level that Woolworth retained after the merger. Kapstein went on to manage several Woolworth stores on the West Coast, but when he was submitted for the important post as a New York buyer by his immediate superiors, he was turned down because of the rife anti-Semitism that existed within the New York executive office. Despite this, he stayed on with the company as manager of its San Francisco store on Market Street from 1922 to 1930. The downtown San Francisco store was one of the most successful stores in the chain, but in 1930 the president of the Woolworth Co. came to the West Coast to inspect the stores and after he toured Kapstein's store, he turned to the district manager and said that "the New York Office had decided that they didn't want a Jew to manage one of the largest stores in the United States."[19] Kapstein was offered a management position in the San Jose store, but by then he had enough, and resigned from the Woolworth Co.

Kapstein went on to form a small chain of Standard five & ten cent stores in the San Francisco Bay area, one of which still exists today on California Street, and he also formed a very successful business called Kay Novelties. The ironic part of this was that the Woolworth stores on the West Coast became one of his best customers.

The surviving correspondence, meager as it is, is more than sufficient to reveal the characteristics of its founder—his diligence, his mastery of his trade, and above all his humanity. As for Kapstein, it shows him as a devoted employee and an eminently decent man. In his unpublished autobiography it was obvious that there was a mutual respect between him and Charlton. It is worth noting that Kapstein never achieved his original wish (as expressed in the letters) to return to the east, but settled permanently in California, where he became an eminently successful merchant and entrepreneur.

After a long and productive life, Simon Kapstein died in California in 1971 at the age of eighty-five. He and his wife Jeannette (Bedrick) had one daughter, Dorothy, and two sons, Dr. John Kerner and Robert (Bob) Kerner, both of whom assisted their father in his businesses in the early days and still reside in the San Francisco Bay area.

---

[19] Quoted from Simon Kapstein's unpublished autobiography.

RULES & DEMANDMENTS OR 10 DEMANDMENTS

1. Don't lie; it wastes my time and yours. I am sure to catch you in the end and that's the *wrong end.*

2. Watch your work not the clock. A long day's work makes a long day short, and a short day's work makes my face long.

3. Give me more than I expect and I'll pay you more than you expect. I can afford to increase your pay if you can increase my profits.

4. You owe so much to yourself that you can't afford to owe anybody else. Keep out of debt or keep out of my store.

5. Dishonesty is never an accident. Good men, like good women, can't see temptation when they meet it.

6. Mind your business and in time you will have a business of your own to mind.

7. Don't do anything here which hurts your self-respect. The employee who is willing to steal from me is capable of stealing from me.

8. It's none of our business what you do at night, BUT if dissipation affects what you do the next day and you do half as much as I demand, you'll last half as long as you hoped.

9. Don't tell what I'd like to hear, but what I'd ought to hear. I don't need a valet to my vanity, but I need one for my dollars.

10. Don't kick if I kick—if you're worthwhile correcting, you're worthwhile keeping. I don't waste time cuffing specks out of rotten apples.

Earle Charlton's "Rules & Demandments or 10 Demandments," though obviously humorous, nonetheless captures his commitment to honesty, integrity, and hard work.

III

THE GREAT MERGER

As CHARLTON'S CHAIN OF 5 & 10 CENT STORES FLOURISHED, particularly in Canada and the west coast of the United States in the early 1900s, the other members of the *friendly* competitors, namely the F. W. Woolworth & Co., C. S. Woolworth, F. M. Kirby, and S. H. Knox, were encountering increasing competition on the east coast from their *not so friendly* competitors, led by S. S. Kresge, S. H. Kress, J. G. McCrory, Titus Supply Co., H. Germain, and Rothchild & Co. By the end of the first decade of the 20th century, the competitive stores who duplicated Frank Woolworth's merchandise mix and prices were opening stores almost as rapidly as were he and his associates. Together, the competition had nearly as many stores as Woolworth himself, namely 319 stores.

Then, around 1906, rumors began circulating of a great merger among these rivals, which, if successful, might even eclipse the great chain Woolworth himself had built. In fact, there was already fierce competition among the various contenders, aimed chiefly at Woolworth, obliging him to reduce prices almost to the giveaway point on some items in order to retain his lead each time his contenders challenged him with their own price cutting. In the end, nothing came of the potential threat, but it surely provided the stimulus for Frank Woolworth to make his own move.

MEGA-MERGER

In April of 1911 he called the members of his loosely federated retail "family" together—his brother Charles, Fred Kirby, Seymour Knox, and

Earle Charlton—for a secret conference at the (old) Waldorf-Astoria Hotel in Manhattan. He proposed a gigantic merger among them. Over the next seven months negotiations proceeded at various sites in New York City, including the Plaza Hotel, and finally concluded five months later at the Woolworth headquarters itself. Negotiations for the amalgamation of the five owners' companies first went slowly, apparently because of Frank Woolworth's insistence that any new entity bear his name alone; this was a major sticking point for those who had laboriously built their own chains, but Woolworth, who had long cherished notions of becoming a commercial Napoleon, held firm. (He later even bought that emperor's desk and used it as his own.)[1] Eventually his will prevailed, and it must have been as a token of concession by the others that they all were in his debt as originator of the five-and-ten concept and its most successful embodiment.

Little has surfaced from the negotiations to reflect the positions of the various vendors, but it would appear that Frank Woolworth must have been generous with them if he wished to make the settlement he actually did. That he was naturally of a generous nature is also suggested by his loyalty to his old benefactor William H. Moore, who by then apparently was not doing well at his original business. At Woolworth's insistence, he was included as one of the vendors in the new merger agreement.

It was not until September 16 that the vendors drafted their preliminary merger agreement; then it took until November 1 for the five to work out and sign the actual document (it came to be known as the "Vendor Agreement"), containing the finer details of the merger, including the location of regional offices, the naming of buyers and managers, the exact apportioning of stocks among the founders and other officers and, of course, salaries.

Announcement of the merger to the general public was made on 2 November 1911. At the same time, details of the giant new company's financial underpinning were divulged: it was to be capitalized at $65,000,000, of which $15,000,000 was to be in preferred stock and $50,000,000 in common stock, the latter to be marketed through Goldman, Sachs & Co.

---

[1] His now-familiar monogram, the "W" in a diamond, even recalls the "N" of the French emperor.

Company officers were to be F. W. Woolworth, as president, with the remainder of the founders designated as vice-presidents. All were appointed as members of the executive committee, and also to terms on the board of directors. A new announcement of the following day, 3 November 1911, also divulged the structure of the new company, creating the executive office at the Stewart Building, 280 Broadway, plus eight district offices to be located in Manhattan, Boston, Wilkes Barre, Buffalo, Toronto, Chicago, St. Louis, and San Francisco.

Stores were each to be given a permanent number in accordance with their ranking in sales for 1911, except that the huge new former S. H. Knox store on State Street in Chicago was to be ranked as no. 1. Thereafter, newly opened stores were to be numbered according to their date of opening.

In addition, the five vendors (founders) were placed on fixed salaries, with $25,000 to Frank Woolworth as president, and $10,000 each to the four remaining founders. But it is apparent that their wealth was hardly to be the result of these salaries, but rather of dividends from their preferred stock. Of this, Earle Perry Charlton received an initial block of more than 30,000 shares, which made him an extremely wealthy man, especially because this stock was constantly being divided.

THE NEW F. W. WOOLWORTH CO.

The new Woolworth Co. was incorporated on 15 December 1911, and Frank Woolworth sent the following general letter to the store managers:

> Regarding store managers, the new arrangement does not affect them any more than if there were no new company to be organized, and we shall make just as few changes in store managers as heretofore.
>
> In the district offices, we have endeavored to mix the men from the various companies in all of the offices so as to make the entire organization as harmonious as possible.
>
> After the first of January, 1912, there will be no so-called Woolworth stores, Knox stores, Kirby stores, Charlton stores, C. S. Woolworth stores or Moore stores. It will be one harmonious whole.

The only exception to the comments in Mr. Woolworth's letter were that the individual or "mother" stores of each one of the five founders would maintain their individual founders name. Thus, the overhead sign for the Charlton store on Main Street in Fall River carried the "E. P. CHARLTON & CO." name until 13 June 1970, when it closed after 62 years in the same location.

At the time of the merger on 1 January 1912, the new F. W. Woolworth Co. contained a total of 596 stores as follows:

Company	Sales (1911)	US stores	Can. stores	Total stores
F. W. Woolworth & Co.	$26,887,035	319		319
S. H. Knox & Co.	$13,047,745	98	13	111
F. M. Kirby & Co.	$7,253,036	96		96
E. P. Charlton & Co.	$4,070,683	35	18	53
C. S. Woolworth	$1,207,849	15		15
W. H. Moore	$149,776	2		2
TOTAL	$52,614,213	565	31	596

Fig. 7. Official portrait (1912) of the founders of the F. W. Woolworth Company (from the left), F.W. Kirby, E.P. Charlton, F.W. Woolworth, C.S. Woolworth, and S.H. Knox. A copy of this portrait was displayed in each Woolworth store throughout the world.

Of the five founders, Frank Woolworth was the least able to enjoy his new status as merchant prince. Shortly after the merger was completed, he suffered a severe nervous breakdown. His physicians ordered him to take a rest cure at the famous Carlsbad (Kárlovy Vary) spa in Bohemia. In the remaining seven years of his life after the merger, he became morose, grossly obese, and brooded over the last object that gave him purpose, construction of the great Woolworth Building at 233 Broadway, which opened in April of 1913.

For Earle Charlton, however, the merger was a happy affirmation of his hard work, an opportunity and a liberation. For him, life was barely starting. Although Charlton retired from the daily operation of the company, he did attend Woolworth board meetings and executive committee meetings at the Woolworth Building in New York City.

Fig. 8. On occasion, Charlton would write articles in his capacity as vice president of the Woolworth Co., one of which, "Mass Selling, An Important Influence," which was published in the *Boston Transcript* in 1929, follows.

Mass Selling:
An Important Influence

By Earle P. Charlton

Big mercantile business would be impossible without it–
example of Woolworth Company–
rapid turnover requires public confidence ...

Napoleon, the greatest military genius of history, once declared: "It is not the size of an army which is most important, but how fast and how steadily that army can be kept moving." It seems to me that the observation of the mighty Corsican—who out-thought his enemies before he out-fought them—might well be taken as the keynote of those two great movements of modern merchandising which we call mass production and mass distribution. Because it does not matter how much we produce nor how large may be our organization—if we are not able to move our product—if we are not able to turn it over fast enough and steadily enough, we shall not be able to continue business.

CONSUMERS ARE DIRECTORS

The larger the organization and the heavier its investment the more is this fact emphasized. The consumers whom it serves are always its superior. The people are always its dictators, its masters. If they do not buy its products and keep on buying those products, it is ruined. And they will not buy unless they have a definite need and a definite desire—unless they are offered a definite economy, a definite quality, or a definite service—or all three.

The F. W. Woolworth Company, called by economists "The Father of Distributors to the Classes and for the Masses," has been built on receipts of nickels and dimes to an annual business of more than $270,000,000 because it has always recognized that no matter how cheap its prices might be made, it could never continue operation unless it could supply definite needs of millions of customers. We are often asked how we are able to sell more than ten thousand separate articles for as little as five or ten cents and make any profit. I have given you the answer. The people make it possible—by how much and how fast they will buy from us. And they will not buy unless they have confidence in what they buy.

The foundation of mass production and mass distribution must be rapid turnover. And this can be built only on public confidence. Without mass selling—not now and then, but all the time—big mercantile business would not be possible. The Woolworth Company may tie up one million dollars in a single order of one product to retail for ten cents, knowing that its profit on any one sale could not be more than a fraction of a cent. But it is banking on the fact that it will not have to wait a year or six months or even three months to turn over this investment.

TURNOVER IN 43 DAYS

It expects a turnover in forty-three days—and each forty-three days thereafter throughout the year. In other words, it will make the same invested capital work for it eight and one-half times in one year. That is why it is able to sell for as low as ten cents through mass production and mass distribution articles which formerly cost the public—with old-fashioned merchandising methods—anywhere from fifty cents to one dollar. But remember the most important fact of all—the moment the public fails to buy from us fast enough and steadily enough, our whole structure crumbles. It would not be the loss of only one investment of one million dollars which I have used as an example, but many.

The F. W. Woolworth Company does a business of nearly one million dollars each working day. This million dollars is contributed by more than ten million people. Without the constant support and co-operation of these ten million people, the Woolworth Company's distribution soon would cease to be possible. Even the tremendous mass production, huge buying power, and the elaborate Woolworth organization spanning five nations would not save it. The most important asset of the F. W. Woolworth Company is not the millions of dollars which enable it to buy and sell at the lowest cash prices—but the confidence of the men, women and children whose nickels and dimes have built its development. Once this confidence is lost, once those nickels and dimes fail to make fast enough trips to the Woolworth counters, an annual business of more than $270,000,000 is shattered. Many factors enter into the mass production and mass distribution of a modem mercantile business: improved machinery, greater efficiency, swifter turnover, more sustained markets, the elimination of waste. If we wish to be highly technical we could extend the list indefinitely.

New Type of Buying Public

But it seems to me that many business men have a tendency to overlook the factor which is more vital than any of these. A new type of buying public has developed within the present generation—more educated, more discriminating, more demanding. The day is over when cheap prices were all that was necessary to attract a crowd. The era of so-called "bargain sales," with the "bargains" more or less imaginary, is gone forever. The buying public of today is not satisfied with something "just as good" because the price is lower. It is concerned with more than the immediate purchase. It wants to know the service it is going to get for the money it is spending. The fact is just as true whether the article costs only five or ten cents or five or ten dollars. And this advance in public education, which now affects every kind of merchandising, can be traced to the influence of mass production and mass distribution of many of the necessities of life.

For example, although Woolworth has brought more varieties of merchandise within the purchasing power of more and more consumers, it has never once permitted a lowering in quality. This has always been emphasized since the early days of Frank Woolworth, when he was a struggling young merchant. That is why the F. W. Woolworth Company spends a large sum of money each year in testing and retesting the quality of what goes on to its counters before the public is invited to buy. We reject many more new articles than we add to our list because they fail to measure up to the quality standards which public education has made necessary.

Such a quality would be impossible at Woolworth prices if it were not for mass production and distribution and swift turnovers. It would be utterly out of the question with the old-time methods of merchants operating entirely as individuals and buying in small quantities. So much the public owes to the tremendous advance of organized merchandising which buys in orders of millions rather than hundreds or even thousands. And it is a public service which I believe is one of the most important which has been rendered to modern life—and which is seldom given its proper emphasis in any consideration of the advantages of mass merchandising.

WHAT EDISON ACCOMPLISHED

About the same time that Frank Woolworth was fighting his discouraging battle to establish his new merchandising idea, another young American was fighting an equally discouraging battle to establish another kind of service. That second young man was Thomas A. Edison. When he perfected an invention to insert the filaments into his new incandescent electric light bulbs by machinery instead of slow and wasteful hand labor, the workmen threatened to mob him, claiming that he was taking away their employment, that they would be out of a job. They did not realize that the young pioneer was putting more money into their pockets; that he was making more employment possible for more people at more money; that instead of cutting down opportunities for labor, he was making infinitely more opportunities at far higher returns. Bear this in mind, for it cannot be repeated too often.

Every factor which tends to increase the consumption of any necessity of life by increasing the production and lowering the cost of manufacturing and marketing means that everything and everybody, directly or indirectly affected, is bound to benefit. That is not theory. It is proven economic fact.

KEYNOTE OF WOOLWORTH SUCCESS

This is why mass distribution and turnover of modern merchandising means not only greater purchasing power but greater saving power and greater earning power for millions of more people. Woolworth success has been built on the idea that its expansion must depend upon the time and labor and money it can save for the largest number of people. This is the kind of service which extends the possibilities of life and which within the past half century has revolutionized much of the physical world in which we live. This is the idea behind mass production and mass distribution and mass turnover.

Told in one sentence, it is the idea that the more the merchant can do for the consumer, the more efficiently he can study and supply the needs of the consumer and the greater will be his own progress and success.

IV

AT HOME WITH THE CHARLTONS

EARLE CHARLTON MARRIED IDA MAY STEIN, of Buffalo, New York, on his twenty-sixth birthday, 19 June 1889. She was the daughter of Karl and Magdalena L. Stein, German merchant immigrants from Baden Baden, a spa town in the Black Forest. Earle almost certainly first met Ida during one of his sales swings through upstate New York during his employment by Newell, from whose service he resigned shortly after his marriage. It seems he then settled temporarily in Buffalo, for the original business alliance with Seymour Knox was signed there on 13 December 1889, and lists both as residents of that city. One can assume from the close timing of marriage and partnership that he did not see fit to venture into matrimony until he had achieved a degree of financial independence and could foresee a more prosperous future than that of a traveling employee. Only two months after signing his agreement with Knox, he brought Ida to Fall River, where he was even then establishing his first store under the Knox-Charlton banner.

Some eighteen months later their eldest child, Ruth, was born on 31 January 1891, followed on 23 August 1893, by Earle Perry, Jr., and on 21 May 1895, by their second daughter, Virginia. By that year, Charlton was prospering, and they had made the decision to move from a modest home at 38 French Street in Fall River to a more substantial, but hardly pretentious, house at 635 Rock Street. From his new home he could commute down the long hill to his office above his original store in the old A. J. Borden Building at 105 South Main Street. One can glimpse him there in 1902 through the eyes of young Simon Kapstein, who approached him soon after graduating from the Fall River High School. Charlton was even then working assiduously to build his Canadian chain and envisioning the establishment of stores in the Far West. Ten years later, of course, he had done all these things and merged with Woolworth—even though his enlarged mother—store by then had moved just down South Main to numbers 91–103 and still proudly bore the name "E. P. Charlton Company" above its display windows. (Above this was a much smaller sign, reading "F. W. Woolworth Co., Successor.")

Fig. 9. The Charlton Building was the headquarters of the E. P. Charlton Co., located in downtown Fall River at 91–93 South Main Street. Accommodating two sales floors, the top floor contained the executive and buying offices. The original Knox & Charlton store was opened a few doors up the street in the Borden Building on February 22, 1890. The new E. P. Charlton & Co. was formed in 1895 and the store was moved to 91–93 Main on February 28, 1908. It was completely remodeled in 1955 (sometime after which this photograph was taken) and closed on June 13, 1970, after 62 years in this location.

Had he wished to do so, after the merger had assured his wealth and position in the business world, Charlton could have moved to New York City and purchased a mansion on Fifth Avenue or in Brooklyn Heights, but the prospect seems never to have appealed to him. Instead, dyed-in-the-wool New Englander that he was, he divided his time between the substantial, but hardly pretentious, house he had purchased on the heights of Rock Street and "Pond Meadow," a grander house he had purchased in the late 1890s from the estate of New York banker and industrialist Henry M. Steers at Acoaxet, Massachusetts, twenty miles south of Fall River on a tiny neck of land at the very corner of the state where the states of Rhode Island and Massachusetts meet bordering Rhode Island Sound. On Sundays, he and Ida attended the great Central Congregational Church on Rock Street in Fall River, or in summer a non-denominational Protestant service held in Acoaxet.

THE FIRST POND MEADOW

His Victorian frame mansion in Acoaxet was the first fruit of his success with his own growing chain, and it seems to have been conceived principally as a summer dwelling. For winter use and for those occasions when he needed to be near his work, he maintained his original dwelling at 635 Rock Street. (It was sold by the family only in the 1930s following his death.)

The Pond Meadow home in its original form endured for less than twenty years after Charlton had purchased it. Just as its first owner, Henry Steers, had met death by drowning while on a fishing expedition nearby, the house itself fared little better. For only three years after its new owner's merger with Woolworth, on 17 April 1915, as it was being painted and remodeled for the summer season, an unexplained fire broke out in the unoccupied wooden dwelling during the evening hours, and the house was totally destroyed, along with part of its gardens. Only a single pair of rubber boots were rescued from the basement by a volunteer. Fortunately, the outbuildings and greenhouses were saved, as were neighboring houses, if only because that evening the wind was light. According to the *Fall River Globe* of that date, the damages amounted to around $60,000, a considerable sum in pre-World War I America. Most of this was insured, but the Charlton family lost all of its fine furnishings not housed on Rock Street, and its members were demoralized by the total loss of their goods and memorabilia.

THE NEW POND MEADOW

Determined this time not to suffer another such loss by fire, just after World War I, Charlton constructed a new, more modem and grander Pond Meadow on virtually the same site. But in architecture and scale it little resembled the earlier home. For one thing, it was twice the size— it occupied 40,000 square feet and encompassed 24 rooms with 9 bathrooms, and this time made as fireproof as possible. It was constructed of Italian marble and great blocks of granite, most two feet wide, transported by barge from quarries in Rhode Island and Maine. To fashion them, masons were imported from Italy. Floors were made of concrete reinforced with steel; they were so solid that whenever repairs or modifications to the plumbing were required, they had to be opened with a jack hammer! To complete the building specifications, the roof was constructed of heavy fireproof slate and this, along with the other construction materials that Charlton insisted on, certainly helped Pond Meadow fend off any of the damage from the great hurricane of 1938 that destroyed most every home located on the beachfront. When completed, the cost approached a half-million dollars.

Fig. 10. Front view of Pond Meadow. The beautifully manicured grounds included a circular pebble driveway that led to the front door.

Fig. 11. View of Pond Meadow from the ocean side. The back lawn was set up as a nine hole "pitch and put" golf course during the summer.

Fig. 12. Earle P. Charlton and one of his many motor cars.

The interior of the home was spectacular. Mahogany was used to panel the interior and for the grand staircase which was the focal point of the home. The staircase, covered with rich red carpeting, was located in the huge entrance hall, a room that served as a greeting room and a family gathering place where the Charlton family spent their evenings by a roaring fire in the Italian marble fireplace (on cold nights) reading, conversing and working on jigsaw puzzles, which was one of Mrs. Charlton's favorite pastimes. Eventually, after Mr. Charlton's death, Mrs. Charlton had an elevator installed which was used by her, almost exclusively, until her death.

The formal living room, mainly used for receptions and parties, was carpeted in a plush off-white carpet and contained beautifully upholstered sofas and chairs, antique tables, a George II antique walnut and parcel-gilt secretary, and two magnificent antique black and gold Chinese lacquered cabinets, one containing a player organ. The pipes for the organ were concealed in the walls of the living room. Just off the living room was a small atrium decorated with plants and flowers.

The formal dining room ceiling was covered in gold leaf, highlighted by lights hidden in a mahogany cornice around the entire room, which gave the room a dramatic effect. The huge George III-style mahogany dining room table, twelve matching tapestry chairs, and eight George I side chairs filled the room, used for formal dinners and banquets. In the comer of the room hiding the pantry door from the diners eyes was an 18th-century ten-panel Coromandel screen. Mr. Woolworth, Mr. Knox, Mr. Kirby, and President Calvin Coolidge and their spouses were among the notables who dined with the Charltons, along with the notable families and friends from Fall River, Acoaxet, Boston, New York, and Newport. The Garden Room, just off the formal dining room, was used for most of the Charlton's meals: breakfast, lunch, and dinner. It was a bright room with many windows, plants, flowers, and a large glass circular table and comfortable chairs. One had the feeling of dining in a garden in a splash of sunlight.

The seven bedrooms upstairs were tastefully appointed with beautiful drapes and bedspreads, comfortable beds, antique nightstands, and ornamental chests of drawers. The walls were decorated with beautiful prints of famous young ladies and gentlemen, such as Pink Lady and Blue Boy. The waste-baskets were all covered with Currier & Ives prints. In the basement there was a bowling alley that was very popular with the young set and a professional billiard table which attracted the men when they had finished their after dinner glass of wine, coffee, and cigars.

The outbuildings on the twenty-two-acre grounds were nearly as remarkable; the carriage house could accommodate six cars and two trucks; during Earle Charlton's lifetime it housed, among other vehicles, two Rolls Royces. Two large greenhouses provided fresh flowers for vases everywhere in the house throughout the year; occupied or not, the interior temperature at Pond Meadow was maintained at a constant 72 degrees Fahrenheit (in later years the annual cost approached $35,000!) The house also had its own water system; water was piped in from a spring-fed pond about a mile distant and stored in an elevated tank. Finally, in addition to their principal compound, the Charltons also owned a farm in Acoaxet, on ground just to the north. It produced vegetables and dairy products for the family. In 1919 the Charltons thus occupied this splendid new dwelling as their principal residence, retaining the Rock Street address chiefly for convenience in inclement weather or for early morning departures by train.

The houses at Rock Street and Acoaxet were hardly the sole Charltonian residences. For his visits to Boston, where he variously served as trustee and director, Charlton leased a spacious apartment at 250 Beacon Street, overlooking the Charles River. It was used by all family members, and was retained by Ida until her death.

QUI-SI-SANA IN PALM BEACH

Meanwhile, in order to escape New England winters, the couple turned to Florida, and they rented a suite at the exclusive Poinciana Hotel in Palm Beach before deciding to build a suitable residence of their own. This occurred in or around 1922, when Charlton purchased a large tract of land, formerly part of the El Bravo estate, and built a splendid two-story mansion, called "Qui-si-Sana," along its oceanfront at El Brillo Way and Ocean Boulevard in the prevailing Florida Iberian style of the period, complete with tile roof and prevailing "Spanish" furniture of the

Twenties.[1] It possessed rustic arcade galleries on the second level, a large colonnaded patio replete with fountain and palm trees, tables and deck chairs on shaded verandas, five bedrooms with baths, and a two-car garage. It remained the family's winter residence until the death of Ida Charlton in 1957.[2]

Figs. 13 and 14. Views of Qui-si-Sana.

---

[1] According to the Palm Beach newspaper, the *Independent,* his intention was to sell off other lots of the tract for development. The name "Qui-si-Sana," incidentally, is not Spanish, but Italian, and means "Here one is restored to health."

[2] The house was sold on September 15, 1958.

During their winter residence at Qui-si-Sana, the Charltons were among the most popular members of the Palm Beach Bath and Tennis Club, and of the Everglades Club, where they gave large dinners. But they most frequently entertained at home, where Ida's floral centerpieces were famous, as was her white costume with white fox collar. She was also an active bridge player, and belonged to the South Shore Bridge Club. Earle and Ida also traveled to Europe, making the traditional grand tour in the summer of 1923.

LIVING AT POND MEADOW

Earle and Ida Charlton lived happily at their mansion in Acoaxet until his death there on 20 November 1930. He so thoroughly identified himself with the peninsula on which he lived that he was even instrumental in founding—and funding—the Acoaxet (Country) Club, replete with a nine-hole golf course, tennis courts, and a well-appointed club house. Its membership consisted (and consists today) of prominent homeowners from the peninsula and immediately surrounding area.

His spouse, Ida, was the family gardening enthusiast there and supervised much of the work on Pond Meadow's grounds, as well as exhibiting her flowers at the garden clubs of Fall River, Newport, and Boston. In Rhode Island, for instance, whose Newport Horticultural Society throughout the 1920s and 30s attracted people from all over New England to its fall flower show, she won special prizes for her orchids, and for her *lilium magnificum*, a rare variety of lily.[3]

The 1915 fire that gutted the original homestead at Pond Meadow, incidentally, had spared her greenhouses, and she was constantly at work in them. Until long after her death these were among the mansion's most conspicuous outbuildings.

In addition to gardening, Ida was a lover of classical music and contributed generously to the Boston Symphony Orchestra. She frequency attended its concerts, and in her latter years used the Charlton apartment on Beacon Street for overnighting after concerts of the orchestra. Until her final illness prevented it, she wintered at Qui-si-sana,

---

[3] In her socially active life, Ida was a member of the Women's Club, the Woman's Union, the Palm Beach Garden Club, the Four Arts Club, and the Gulf Stream Club, the Woman City Club of Boston, and the Brookline Country Club.

but Pond Meadow remained her favorite place of residence. She died at the Truesdale Hospital in Fall River on 30 August 1957, aged 88.

Fig. 15. Ida S. Charlton standing at the front gate of Qui-si-Sana with Asko.

THE CHILDREN: RUTH, EARLE JR., AND VIRGINIA

The Charlton children, Ruth, Earle Perry, Jr., and Virginia for all practical purposes grew up in Fall River and summered at the old Pond Meadow. By the time the splendid new Pond Meadow was completed after World War I, Ruth and Virginia's primary interests were elsewhere, and their visits during Earle Charlton's lifetime were confined to the very hot summer months on the promontory (Pond Meadow must have seemed all too remote for young people after going away to school.) Perry, however, spent a great deal of time at Pond Meadow and at Hyannis on Cape Cod.

RUTH CHARLTON MITCHELL MASSON

After her graduation from Dana Hall Preparatory School in Wellesley, Massachusetts, Ruth attended Wellesley, and later Chevy Chase College in Maryland. In one of the great social events of the season, she married Frederick ("Fritz") Mitchell, of Philadelphia,[4] at the original Pond Meadow in June 1914 before going to live in his hometown, Philadelphia. Later, she and her husband purchased a farm in Concordville/Glen Mills, Pennsylvania, which they named "Fox Valley Farms," and where they bred jumpers and hunters as show horses and even created the Mitchell Cup, a competition of their own at the Devon Horse Show, which is still awarded annually.

In the late 1920s the Mitchells returned to Acoaxet, and Earle Charlton built an imposing English-style summer home for them on the Charlton beachfront property. It became one of the showplaces of the peninsula, though one which did not long survive. The great hurricane of 1938 destroyed it, as it did so many homes there. Undaunted, they constructed the stately stone lighthouse that still stands above the great rocks at Pond Meadow, using some of the woodwork in its interior salvaged from their ruined structure. Shortly afterwards, they purchased the home of Judge Morton which was adjacent to the Pond Meadow

---

[4] Fritz Mitchell's family was from Philadelphia and was in the wholesale leather business, trading as Mitchell & Peirson at Gray's Ferry Leather Works. Mitchell was quite successful and left an estate of about $2,000,000 and a stamp collection that was sold at auction for $1,000,000.

property. It was appropriately called the "White House," after its painted exterior, and served as their residence while they summered at the harbor and traveled between Acoaxet and their farm in Glen Mills, Pennsylvania.

Fig. 16. Ruth Charlton Mitchell Masson (1891–1995), the oldest daughter of the Charlton family, carried on the tradition of philanthropy after her parents passed away. Her second marriage, to the noted Mayo Clinic physician Dr. James C. Masson, gave her the incentive to direct a major part of her philanthropic gifts to the Mayo Clinic.

Five years after Mr. Mitchell's death in 1960, Ruth married their close friend and Ruth's personal physician Dr. James C. Masson, a prominent surgeon at the Mayo Clinic who had worked alongside both Will and Charlie Mayo in the early days of the clinic in Rochester, Minnesota. Their marriage took place at Pond Meadow, where they resided for a couple of summers before moving to Rochester. After moving to Rochester, Ruth returned to Acoaxet only twice, once to go over the negotiations for the naming of Charlton Memorial Hospital in Fall River, and for her funeral in 1995. Dr. Masson passed away on 7 December 1972 at the age of 91. Ruth died on 11 February 1995, at the age of 104. She did not have any children.

Even after her death Ruth Masson would be remembered at Mayo, for she left eighty percent of her estate to the Mayo Clinic Foundation, much of which culminated with the construction of the magnificent Charlton Building, a 200,000 square foot structure located at the clinic. The Charlton Building contains one of the largest cancer radiation and nuclear medicine centers in the world, and five additional stories were constructed and opened in 1999. (See chapter 7 for a complete list of the contributions that Mrs. Masson made to Mayo and the Mayo Medical School. There is no doubt that Ruth's father had instilled his charitable influence in her.)

EARLE PERRY, JR.

The son, Earle Perry, Jr., who preferred to be called Perry, attended several schools, including Amherst College, for a time, but showed little interest in academic courses and never completed his degree. Later he moved to Boston before returning to Fall River, where he became a cotton broker and even worked for a time as a banker.

If not interested in courses at Amherst, he showed keen interest in courses of another variety—golf courses—and became one of the better amateur (left-handed) players in the area. He competed up and down the coast and at White Sulphur Springs with the Acoaxet golf pro Ed Phinney, and occasionally played the likes of Gene Sarazen, Frank Stranahan, Sam Snead, and others, usually for money. His marriage to Elizabeth C. Moore, of Medford, Massachusetts, did not long endure, but he had two children by her: a daughter, Thelma, and a son Earle Perry II, both of whom were raised in the west from the early 30s, but summered at Pond Meadow.[5] After his mother Ida's death in 1957, Perry moved into Pond Meadow and occupied it during the summers until his own passing at the age of 79 on 7 June 1973 in the Charlton Surgery Wing of the Truesdale Hospital after a lengthy illness.[6]

Fig. 17. Earle Perry Charlton with two of his grandchildren in 1930: Earle P. Charlton II (co-author of this book) and Thelma Charlton (West).

---

[5] Thelma prefers to be called "Teddy." She, her husband Col. Fraser E. West of Reno, Nevada and their children, Christina, Karen, Sondra, and Bill, live on a cattle ranch in Ione, California. Earle II, known as "Chuck," his wife Frances (Acker) of San Mateo, California and their daughter, Stacey Lynn, reside in Hillsborough, California.

[6] Earle Perry Charlton, Jr. provided Truesdale Hospital in Fall River with new ambulances whenever they were needed.

VIRGINIA CHARLTON LINCOLN

Virginia, after graduation from the Bennett School and Pine Manor College, set out for an around-the-world-tour in 1919 with a former teacher and a chum, Kathleen Phillips, returning via Hawaii and San Francisco. They visited everything from World War I trenches to a riot against British rule in Cairo, the men's smoking room of the Topkapi Palace in Istanbul, and Ghandi's ashram in Ahmedabad. They even dared to visit Manchuria during the civil war there, where her teacher, Miss Sherwood, was struck with a quirt en route to Mukden by a Chinese soldier when she attempted to photograph a passing troop train. Soon after her return, Virginia married Kenneth Lincoln, a builder, moved to Arlington, Massachusetts, and settled down to a far less adventurous life there. She was very generous with individuals down on their luck, and performed numerous acts of impromptu charity. Prior to 1938 the Lincolns also spent summers at their house, on the grounds of Pond Meadow, which along with that of the Mitchells was destroyed in 1938. They had four children, two of whom died shortly after birth: Earle, who died at an early age, and Dr. Henry Lincoln, who later became a physician and practiced medicine at the Truesdale Hospital in Fall River (which during his tenure had become the Charlton Memorial Hospital). Virginia lived to the age of 87, and died in October 1982.[7]

HOUSEHOLD STAFF

Perhaps the most colorful of Earle Charlton's household staff at Pond Meadow was an Italian from Como named Luigi (or Louis) Perini. He had originally been hired at age fourteen by Frank Woolworth to act as his personal valet,[8] but as it turned out no provision was made for him on Woolworth's death, and the story told by Charlton himself, following the great man's funeral at the palatial Winfield House on Long Island, Charlton spotted Louis sitting on the staircase, head in hands, a picture of

---

[7] Virginia Lincoln provided a new layette to every new baby born at Truesdale Hospital for many years.

[8] Woolworth put Louis in charge of keeping his bedroom refrigerator well stocked at all times with all of his favorite foods and drinks. An insomniac, Woolworth would awaken several times during the night and ingest huge quantities of food.

dejection. He was not only sad at the death of his master, but he asked Charlton "What is to become of me? I have lost my sponsor and there is nothing for me now but to return to Italy!"

Upon hearing this, Charlton asked Louis if he would like to work for him and hired him on the spot, telling him to go to the Manhattan office of the Old Fall River Steamship Line, where there would be a ticket awaiting him, and that a chauffeur would meet him at the dock in Fall River for the trip to Pond Meadow. Thereafter he served the Charlton family as butler and major-domo uninterruptedly for sixty years, or until his death in 1979. He was known by everyone visiting the Charltons, from President Calvin Coolidge to heads of corporations and charities, visitors from New York, Washington, and Palm Beach. Louis, in return, knew them all and served them his famous ice tea, whose formula he long kept secret.

LOUIS'S FAMOUS ICED TEA RECIPE

In a letter dated 12 April 1971 to E. P. Charlton II, Louis Perini divulged his hitherto-secret recipe for his celebrated iced tea drink. Everyone who came to Pond Meadow or Qui-si-Sana for lunch or afternoon tea knew about Louis's iced tea, but he would never give out his secret recipe. He kept a good supply of the iced tea in Poland Water Bottles in the pantry, and many a family member or guest would be seen peeking into the refrigerator to see if the delicious nectar was available.

No one was allowed inside Pond Meadow without clearance from Louis, and it is reputed that vendors had to present him with tokens of their esteem in order to do business. During the 1930s Louis married Ruth Lofgren, the Pond Meadow upstairs maid, who was Swedish. Others from this period were George Donnelly, an Irishman, and Charlton's longtime chauffeur of his Rolls Royces, Anna McGillivray, also from Ireland, as head chef, and Louise Carlson, Anna McDonough, and George Cook.

Louis Perini's Famous Iced Tea Recipe

Iced Tea (2 quarts)

Take 8 (or 10 if you prefer) flow-through bags of tea (your choice). Put in an enamel pitcher. Pour over this 3 pints of hot boiling water; simmer for ten minutes or until the tea is strong.

Add: 8 (or 10 oz.) lemon juice and pulp, not rind.

4 oz. grapefruit juice and pulp, not rind

2 cup granulated sugar (or to your taste). Strain—let it cool before putting in refrigerator. [Perini called this mixture his "syrup." He explained, "This … can be kept in the refrigerator in a sealed bottle or container for days."]

Half fill glasses with ice when serving. This can also be served hot—1/2 cup "syrup" & 1/2 cup hot water."

[Louis would be the first one to tell you that his ice tea recipe was not meant for "weight watchers" and diabetics!]

At a later date, John Kelly would replace George Donnelly as the Charlton's chauffeur, and Mary O'Brien would become the family's personal secretary, but all in all the staff was fiercely loyal to the Charltons and stayed with them for the best period of their lives, and the Charltons, both Earle and Ida, took good care of them in their wills and, in some instances, with the help of the First National Bank of Boston, set up trusts for the members of the staff and their spouses. Everett Petty was the head groundskeeper for the Pond Meadow estate, and he had a staff of up to five gardeners to keep the grounds immaculate at all times, the miles of hedges trimmed, the acres of lawn mowed, the pea gravel raked every day, the fresh vegetables ready to be harvested, and the flowers in the greenhouses in bloom for the numerous flower arrangements adorning the main house. During the existence of the old Pond Meadow mansion, staff members were housed in a separate—and very comfortable—building nearby, and walked to Pond Meadow for their work. After the fire, household employees received quarters in the new Pond Meadow building, in two long corridors above its kitchen, while chauffeurs and groundskeepers were separately housed in other buildings on the grounds.

ASKO, A CHAMPION AND A HERO!

No chapter on family and housing could be complete without mention of Earle Charlton's prize-winning German shepherd dog, Asko von Pasewalk, P.H. (for Polizei Hunde). Asko had been born in 1921 and trained in Germany by a noted dog handler, Fritz Wolff, as a working police dog. Asko learned absolute obedience, and was even trained to kill on his master's utterance of a secret command. He was imported as a puppy by a prominent physician and Rock Street neighbor of the Charltons, Dr. P. H. Walsk, who began displaying him at meetings of the American Kennel Club. He first won prizes as best of his breed at Taunton in 1923, then went on to a series of regional—and finally national—dog shows, where as representative of the Naragansett Kennels he ultimately amassed 73 ribbons. His crowning triumph came in 1924, when judged by a panel of twenty-one experts, he defeated dogs from Germany, Great Britain, and France, including the reigning French shepherd dog Yvonne de Beauchamps. He was thereupon proclaimed national champion in his class.

Shortly thereafter, Dr. Walsh presented him to Earle Charlton, where Asko became his constant companion, even accompanying him and Ida to Palm Beach on their winter travels. But the dog's distinguished career was scarcely finished. Two years later, in 1926, Billy Harticon, three-year-old son of William F. Harticon, a mill supplier who summered in Westport, disappeared with a pet Blue Setter from the family house in Stonington, Connecticut. The trail led to the edge of Miners' Swamp, and was lost. A full day went by, with no trace of the missing child.

Billy's father frantically appealed to Charlton and to the owners of other trained police dogs. Charlton quickly turned Asko over to Dr. Walsh, who, accompanied by Louis Perini, rushed the dog to Stonington. Before starting, Dr. Walsh also contacted a dog trainer named Holden who lived near Fall River and owned Fritz, Asko's purebred son. They also appealed to the owner of another trained police dog named Caesar, though Caesar and his master lived at too great a distance to join the other dogs in time.

Holden gave Asko and Fritz the scent of Billy's clothing, and the little posse plunged into the swamplands to no immediate avail. No single scent must have seemed positive enough to the animals, who even separated and followed different trails for a time. By 6:30 in the evening, the seekers were beginning to fear for the worst when, exhausted, the dogs doubled back to a trail they had followed earlier. Men and dogs were then obliged momentarily to rest. At that moment a faint cry was heard from a thicket. The rescuers crashed through the undergrowth and found Billy clinging to his Blue Setter.

Billy's arms and legs were badly scratched from brambles, his face was stained purple from eating wild blueberries, and he was badly dehydrated (even the dogs refused to drink from the fetid black waters of the swamp). Billy and his dog were then carried home in triumph, and the good news of their eleventh-hour rescue was broadcast far and wide. Billy's only explanation: "I ran away!"

Asko thus proved himself a hero as well as a show dog, and he spent the remainder of his long life at Earle Charlton's side, and after his master's death at that of his wife, Ida. The Charlton grandchildren remember him well as an affectionate and permissive companion, whose secret command to kill never had to be invoked.

FOUR *EDAMENAS*

Not long before his merger with Woolworth, Earle Charlton acquired a powerboat he called the *Edamena* after his wife, Ida. Then just prior to World War I he acquired a still larger powerboat, a forty-footer which he named *Edamena II*. It was equipped with diesel engines and could reach the speed of twenty knots. When war was declared, Charlton patriotically offered it to the Coast Guard, which logged 4,465 miles on it in 205 days (and blew out one cylinder) before returning it to its owner with thanks. After the war, he purchased two other yachts, the *Edamena III,,* of which rather little is known, save that it was a slightly smaller version of the majestic *Edamena IV,* designed by Walter McGinnis and built at the Peirce & Kilburn shipyards in New Bedford. The *Edamena IV* was 99 feet in length and made its maiden voyage on 27 July 1926; Charlton

moored it his own hundred-foot pier[9] below Pond Meadow on the
Westport River that he had constructed to accommodate the magnificent
new yacht. Besides four staterooms for guests, *Edamena IV* sported a
large lounge and dining area beneath the pilot house, complete with
curtains, tables, overstuffed chairs, a desk, and a bar. On the fantail was
another lounge where the Charltons entertained their guests when the
weather was warm and sunny.[10]

Figs. 18 and 19. Edamena II (above) in 1915 and Edamena IV (below) in 1926. Note the
Coast Guard sailors on the Edamena II, and E. P. Charleton standing amidship on the
Edamena IV.

---

[9] At this writing, it still exists and is known as the Charlton Wharf.

[10] The yacht's name was supposedly taken from a Latin translation: Ida May = Eda +
Mae-na.

The *Edamenas*, II, III, and IV, were certainly large enough to have made the trip down the Atlantic Coast to Palm Beach and back, though there is no record to substantiate that the family ever sailed them between their two oceanfront homes. (If they had done so, the Charltons could have berthed the vessels at the Palm Beach Yacht Club, of which they were also members.) Except for the service of *Edamena II* in World War I, the Charlton yachts seem to have been operated between Acoaxet, Boston, and New York, and included numerous trips to Newport, Buzzards Bay, and Marblehead. Charlton loved to take guests out to view the America's Cup Races off Newport from his yacht. America's *Ranger* and Great Britain's *Endeavor* would provide exciting races, and the American boats would always win the cup!

In New York, Charlton was a member of the prestigious New York Yacht Club,[11] and when the yachts were moored there, he liked to entertain friends on board, including members of his Woolworth family. Unfortunately, Charlton had only four years to enjoy the *Edamena IV* before his death in November 1930. The last cruise that he made on that boat, according to the log book, was on 24 September 1930. The *Edamena IV* was sold two years after his death to a Boston businessman.

POND MEADOW AT AUCTION

In 1977 Ruth Charlton Mitchell Masson was convinced by her private banker that it was no longer feasible to keep Pond Meadow, as she still had the White House across the street, and she was now living in Rochester, Minnesota, with her second husband, Dr. James C. Masson. Monthly bills for keeping up the estate were very high: the heating bill had reached $35,000 a year to keep the interior of the house at 72 degrees all year, and annual real estate taxes were $30,000–$40,000. The maintenance on the house was getting out of hand as it was in constant need of painting, and the slate roof was deteriorating. The outside gardens were not being maintained, as most of the groundkeepers had left or passed on. Only Everett Petty was left, and he was getting on in

---

[11] At the time of E. P. Charlton's membership, the New York Yacht Club membership included the likes of J. P. Morgan, Cornelius Vanderbilt, Whitney, Vincent Astor, and the Rockefellers.

years. The beautiful walkways and neatly trimmed miniature hedges were abandoned to the elements, as were the gardens and trees. It was heartbreaking to see beautiful Pond Meadow unoccupied and neglected. The family had considered giving the estate to the Coast Guard at one time, but they were not interested, and Acoaxet was zoned for residences only. The bank put the estate up for sale and did an aggressive job of trying to sell the estate, including advertising in *Town & Country* and the *Wall Street Journal,* but at that time there was very little interest in a home of that size.

Finally, in 1977, the estate was sold for a paltry sum of $375,000, considerably less than what it cost to build! The new owners, flushed with their great buy, sold several lots off the estate and proceeded to slice Pond Meadow up into five condominiums. Not only did they deface the beautiful home, but they were not even very successful in selling the units. Today Pond Meadow still stands on the point where Rhode Island Sound meets the Westport River, majestic and proud, but badly in need of repairs, painting, and groundskeeping.

THE AUGUST AUCTION

The auction to sell the contents of Pond Meadow took place at Acoaxet on 19–20 August 1977. Two huge circus-type tents were set up on the front lawn, and William Doyle Galleries of New York conducted the two-day auction. Mr. Doyle stated that "about 7,000 people attended the exhibition that preceded the auction," which exceeded everyone's expectations, and about 3,500 people attended the auction, who wanted to see the inside of the beautiful estate and, if they were fortunate enough, to bid for a piece of history. As the auction started, it was obvious that serious bidders were in the crowd. An 18th-century Louis XV French Provincial two-drawer serpentine-front commode went for $2,750, an antique American curly maple slant-front desk brought the same, as did an antique Louis XV French Provincial child's chair; a pair of antique Chinese lacquer cabinets sold for $9,000. The 18th-century ten-panel Coromandel (Chinese) screen went for $16,000, a George III mahogany revolving book table went for $1,900, a 422-piece Reed & Barton Sterling silver Francis I pattern flatware left the estate for $13,000, the George III silver five-piece tea and coffee service (Emes &

Barnard, London, 1819) went for $4,000, a Waltham mahogany 9-tube clock sold for $2,500, a collection of 13 pairs of Dorothy Doughty birds went for as much as $4,500 a pair, a collection of 25 miniature birds by the late A. E. Crowell of East Harwich sold for as much as $2,000 each, an 18th-century Gobelins tapestry brought $6,000, and many paintings and oriental rugs went for various bids from $2,500 to $10,000. When the auction was almost over, on the second day, some of the many bidders and spectators were unhappy that they had not been able to take a piece of Pond Meadow back home with them, so Doyle's auctioneers started cutting up the dark velvet dining room drapes in small pieces so that the people who were still in the tent could purchase a part of Pond Meadow for $10 a piece.

When the auction ended, the auctioneer, William Doyle, stated that it was "probably one of the most successful house sales" that he could remember. He said that "3,500 persons attended the auction, including dealers and collectors from Italy, Paris, Texas and California." Doyle added that the 7,000 people who attended the exhibition preceding the auction must have set a record for attendance in the area. The final sale total, when the receipts were counted, was $530,000, considerably more than the entire 22-acre estate had sold for at $375,000. The entire proceeds of the sale went into the Ruth Charlton Mitchell Charitable Trust, and is currently being used for charitable grants and gifts.

So ended Charlton's 77 years of ownership of Pond Meadow. It had been not only a home for the family, but a meeting place for presidents, business associates, out-of-town guests, friends, and family gatherings. Mrs. Charlton enjoyed hosting beautiful lawn parties surrounded by newly cut flower arrangements from her greenhouses and the ladies sipping on cold glasses of Louis's famous Iced Tea. Mr. Charlton enjoyed having friends down to "the harbor" for a round of golf at the Acoaxet Country Club, or a cruise on his beautiful yacht, *Edamena*. It was truly a time, now long past, for elegance and reflection.

V

SWEET SUCCESS

FOLLOWING THE GREAT MERGER WITH WOOLWORTH, at the age of forty-eight, Earle Charlton was in the unique position to do exactly as he pleased. He had become a wealthy and privileged member of society, a multi-millionaire as director and vice-president in the largest variety store chain of the world. He was handsome and universally admired, sought-after by socialites and business magnates alike. Unlike many men who had worked tirelessly and single-mindedly into middle age to create business empires, he neither paused to loaf and admire his achievements, nor to work repetitively at familiar tasks, but he entered into dozens of new activities, some commercial, some social, and many charitable. These included employment on the directorates of banks, universities, railroads, and social organizations; and during World War I service to his country. Above all, he worked tirelessly for charity.

He possessed that rarest of capacities: the ability to carry many things at once, and any attempt to follow his career year-by-year for the last two decades of his life would merely prove confusing because he moved so quickly from one activity to another. Instead, let us divide his activities into business, service, country, and charity, and then consider them individually.

It goes almost without saying that his position as vice-president of the F. W. Woolworth Co. was foremost among his interests, but it did not require anything like his full time. He continued to live in Massachusetts, and merely entrained occasionally from Fall River via Providence to New York in order to meet with his fellow directors and help determine the future course of the company. He served on both its board of directors and executive committee from the merger until the time of his death in 1930. Had he wished, he might have succeeded Frank

Woolworth as president after his death in 1919, for of the vice-presidents only he and Seymour Knox were of suitable caliber to manage the great enterprise. But Knox had died in 1915, and after Woolworth's own death the company thereafter employed presidents from outside the "family circle." But Earle Charlton was clearly not interested in serving the company in any full-time capacity, especially when the merger had given him *carte blanche* to follow his own star. Rather, as early as 1910, while still planning and expanding his own chain of stores, he branched out in yet another direction and became an industrialist. For all the while he was busy expanding his stores on the West Coast, he was involved in the organization and financing of the ambitious Charlton Mill.

Fig. 20. Earle P. Charlton at the height of his success.

THE CHARLTON MILL

The last and largest of eight new mills constructed in Fall River between 1907 and 1911, the idea for the Charlton mill had originated with a local businessman, James Sinclair, who had grown up in and around textile factories and had become head bookkeeper at Wampanoag Mills. Between 1908 and 1909 he approached a number of Fall River notables with his project for a mill devoted to production uniquely of cotton cloths of the finest quality. Charlton quickly became its most enthusiastic organizer, its largest investor, and subsequently its president. Sinclair was appointed as its secretary-treasurer and selling agent.

The building that housed it was constructed in 1910, and still stands on the southeast corner of Howe and Crawford Streets, on the west shore of Cook Pond. It is a large (154' x 374') solid mill building, its weave shed three stories high, constructed entirely of solid blocks of gray granite. It was of advanced design for its times and its enormous window area and long row of gabled skylights. This great building was accompanied by two smaller ones, also of stone: a powerhouse with tall chimney, and a long, two-story storage shed or warehouse. One can perceive the practical mind of Charlton at work: not only was it solidly constructed, but all the stone needed for its walls was quarried on the twelve acre property, doubtless at a considerable saving over the purchasing and shipping of stone quarried from other sites.[1]

On its ground floor was the carding machinery, with a capacity of 130 cards to feed the weaving "mules" on the second floor. All twelve pairs of mules were of the latest sort and imported from England; together, they comprised 20,352 spindles. Then, sharing the top floor, were situated the ring spinning, the spooling, and the warping departments. Power for the machinery itself was supplied by an enormous compound steam engine weighing 388,000 lbs., while electricity for the frames was generated by a turbine of 900 horsepower.[2] When complete, the plant had a capacity of 90,000 spindles.

Obviously this was no minor undertaking, and it represented a huge investment. Only three years after the mill went into production, America experienced a postwar recession, and many textile mills were operating

---

[1] It is now on the approved list of the National Register of Historic Buildings.

[2] Which made it one of the first mills of its kind to be powered both by steam and by electricity.

only at half capacity. The Charlton mill, however, with its new and more efficient machinery, was able to operate at greater economies than its competitors, and continued to prosper, as it did until after his death in 1930 and even into the Depression. It continued to operate, though not under Charlton family leadership, until the 1950s.

DIRECTORSHIPS

Earle Charlton was now famous in New England, not only as a Woolworth vice-president, but in light of his mill entrepreneurship, as an industrialist. Because of his obvious business acumen, he was approached more and more to take part in the management of businesses from railroads to utilities, although he turned most of them down, if only to conserve his time. But among the most prominent boards that he served on were those of the Eastern Massachusetts Street Railway Co., and of the New York, New Haven & Hartford Railway, where he was named in 1923 to fill the vacancy of the recently deceased director Charles H. Choate, Jr. Charlton had long been a major stockholder of the railroad, and stuck with it in the mid 20s, when the line experienced hard financial times. Credited with having helped to revamp its management, and encouraged by his example, others were persuaded to invest. By his death in 1930, he held a record 17,000 shares, and the railroad was out of difficulty. He also became a director of three banks, the First National Bank of Boston, the National Exchange Bank, of Providence, and the B. M. C. Durfree Trust of Fall River. He also served as a director of the Postum Cereal Co.

Beyond these purely commercial directorships, in 1925 he was named by President John A. Cousens to the Tufts University Board of Trustees, once again, as in the case of the New Haven Railroad, to fill an unexpired term. The honor, he said, gave him great satisfaction, to serve an educational process he personally had been obliged to forsake so early in his career. Before he died, Charlton set up a sizable trust for Tufts University.

CLUB MEMBERSHIPS

As mentioned earlier, Charlton was one of the founders and principal backers of the Acoaxet Club in his summer home location, where the annual Charlton Cup is still the top honor in golf at the club. He was also a member of the Brookline Country Club and the Algonquin Club in Boston, as well as the Gulf Stream Country Club in Palm Beach. Also mentioned earlier was his membership in the prestigious New York Yacht Club, where the America's Cup was proudly displayed. Business affiliations included both the Metropolitan and Bankers Club of Boston, and he was a founding member of the Quequechan Club in Fall River. Charlton was a dedicated member of the Masons, and achieved the 32nd degree. A fervent Republican, he was a close friend of Calvin Coolidge, and spent many days in Washington, often staying in the White House.

WARTIME SERVICE

Earle Charlton did not wait for American entry into World War I to aid the allied cause. Already in 1914 he had generously aided French war relief committees both with time and contributions; moreover his mill loomed cloth for its armies from the beginning of that great conflict. For his help, in 1924, the French government awarded him the *Médaille de la Reconnaissance Française, Argent*. In that same year, when it was known he was about to visit France, the French consul at Boston sent a letter to the Quay d'Orsay, urging that Charlton be shown all possible honors on his arrival in Paris, as indeed he was.

When the United States entered the conflict, Charlton plunged into the raising of money for the war effort in the form of the four liberty loans sponsored by the Treasury. Almost simultaneously President Wilson named him to the War Industries Board; he was later asked by the government to help record its activities for the National Archives. Finally, the competent service he had given to the Board led to his appointment—on 2 November 1918—as director of the Administrative Division of the War Department, with instructions that he should revise its general purchasing policies. To further his authority, the letter of nomination offered him his choice either of suitable military rank or a special civilian status. Of course, before such could be determined, the Germans sued for peace, and an armistice was declared only nine days afterwards. It is not known whether he ever took up this office, but in light of the rapid disarmament that followed the Armistice, it is unlikely. As previously mentioned, Charlton also offered his yacht, the *Edamena II*, to the Coast Guard for service during World War I, and they made good use of it before returning it with thanks (and a blown cylinder).

CHARITY BEGINS AT HOME

The hospital in Fall River, built by Dr. Philemon Truesdale, had been growing gradually since its establishment on another site in 1905. In 1909 it had moved to its present location, and in 1916 been chartered as a community hospital, with Dr. Truesdale acting for the duration of his lifetime in lieu of a board of directors. In 1915, a nurses' residence had been constructed (later to be designated the Mitchell House, after Charlton's daughter Ruth), and in 1923, a south wing was added to the main building, to whose construction and outfitting Charlton had already contributed $35,000. But his role in the construction of the hospital to serve the growing community was only starting. In February 1926 he wrote the following letter from his winter home in Palm Beach to Dr. Truesdale:

> Dear Dr. Truesdale:
>
> My confidence in your able staff and my desire to be of continual help to my community prompt this gift. I have the greatest admiration for the work you have already accomplished and feel sure that with the aid enclosed, greater achievements may be obtained. With this I send my best wishes and appreciation of the many sacrifices you have made for the good of humanity.
>
> Yours sincerely
> Earle P. Charlton

The amount was $500,000, until that time, the largest contribution ever made to any institution in New England, and to contemporaries a staggering amount. The plan was to add a north wing, to match the previously built structures, also three stories high with basement and sub-basement, consisting of a completely equipped laboratory, plus storage, recovery, and operating rooms. Undoubtedly echoing Charlton's previous experience with the blaze at Pond Meadow in 1915, the building was to be completely fireproof. It might be added that he also donated a large and impressive ambulance, complete with spare wheels on the front fenders.[3] Appropriately, Dr. Truesdale announced it would be known as the Earle P. Charlton Surgery and Laboratory Building.

The magnitude of the gift immediately elicited the praise of Fall River's leading citizens, many of whom wrote personal thank-you notes. Said one: "It is a great thing to realize as you do the great responsibility which goes with the acquisition of wealth and Fall River may well be profoundly grateful that you consider money as a means to a service of such inestimable value to its unfortunates." Wrote another: "I never envy a man his riches other than for one thing and that is the ability to make gifts of this kind." He even received grateful letters from people as far away as Boston. Boston, incidentally, had other reasons to be grateful to Charlton: soon afterwards, he contributed $50,000 to the New England Medical Centre's own drive for funds.

PRESIDENT CALVIN COOLIDGE AND CHARLTON

Earle Charlton had not yet exhausted his charitable impulses with his gift to the Truesdale Hospital and the Boston Medical Centre. As an active Republican, he became acquainted with Calvin Coolidge when still governor of Massachusetts. After Coolidge became Vice-President and upon the death of Warren Harding moved into the White House, the two exchanged frequent correspondence, and Charlton was invited on several occasions to visit Coolidge, both in Washington and at his summer White House in upper New York State. One can easily appreciate that they were men of similar Yankee backgrounds and values, and perceive why they became fast friends, though Coolidge certainly outdid Charlton in his famous taciturnity. A long letter from Coolidge seldom exceeded two paragraphs on a single page.

Several letters and notes with "The White House, Washington," dated from 1927 to 1929, are still extant, and they confirm the close relationship that Mr. and Mrs. Charlton had with President and Mrs. Coolidge.

---

[3] Subsequent ambulances for the Truesdale Hospital were contributed by Earle Perry, Jr.

Fig. 21. President Calvin Coolidge and Earle P. Charlton in Washington, D.C., 1928.

In a letter, dated 25 October 1927, Grace Coolidge wrote to Mrs. Charlton expressing her regrets that she and the President could not join the Charltons for a social gathering.

While staying at the White House, Mr. Charlton wrote the following note to Mrs. Charlton on 2 March 1929:

> Darling,
>
> Thought that you would like a line from the White House. State car to meet me, two uniformed men, placed at my disposal. Rose Room suite in front of house and am only guest, others come tomorrow. Am calling you and Ruth up tonight.
>
> Lovingly, Earle

On 6 September 1926 Charlton wrote the following letter to his oldest daughter, Ruth Mitchell, from the White House:

Dear Ruth,

Mrs. Coolidge insists I remain over and meet the Ambassador from Mexico, Sheffield. She has secured nice drawing room for New York, Tuesday night. George back to Boston Woods for Ida. Sorry she did not come. No one here today, but your Dad. Play golf with Cal this afternoon. Will tell you about it when I see you. Arrived Sunday, leaving Tuesday night. President [Coolidge] wants me to come and stay at camp.

Lovingly, Dad

On February 22, 1929, Calvin Coolidge wrote to Charlton to express his desire that Charlton visit him in the White House one more time before Coolidge's departure from office. The two men were to remain fast friends until Charlton's untimely death.

THE PRESIDENT, CHARLTON, AND THE CLARKE SCHOOL FOR THE DEAF

Before her marriage to Coolidge in 1905, his wife Grace had taught at the Clarke School for the Deaf, in Northampton, Massachusetts. The institution ever remained dear to their hearts after their climb to political prominence, and in 1928, as his presidential term approached its end, Coolidge approached Charlton, and asked him if he would be willing to lead a fund raising drive for the school. Charlton—always deeply interested in the ill and handicapped—of course willingly took on the project, and in November 1928 he announced at a White House luncheon that he and Coolidge's other friends had not only formed a committee to raise $2,000,000 for needed new buildings and a research department at the school, but that half had already been raised, thanks to large contributions by Andrew Mellon, William Boyce Thompson, Fred M. Kirby, Clarence Barron, Cyrus Curtis, Edward S. Harkness, and a host of other prominent Americans of the time. To set an example, Charlton personally contributed $110,000. Even Will Rogers lent his moral support in a letter of November 22 to the *New York Times*, observing that the Coolidges were more concerned with the school than in providing for their own support. (It is not known with certainty whether he backed his epistle with modest emoluments, though he almost certainly did.) In any event, Charlton had raised the additional half by December 1928, and Mrs. Coolidge was able to present the school with a check for the full

$2,000,000 even before her husband left office. Charlton termed deafness "one of the most widespread and distressing disabilities of life."

VI

THE CLOSING DAYS

IT WAS ALMOST 1929, by the time the Coolidge Fund had met its goal, when Earle Charlton merited a well-earned rest from activities on behalf of others. He certainly maintained a full-enough docket, considering his rounds of directorial meetings. By February 1930, when he and Ida repaired to Qui-si-Sana in Palm Beach, he intended to socialize and play. But things did not go well with his health. He became suddenly ill at his residence with an undisclosed bladder ailment—probably involving the prostate—and was operated on by a prominent local surgeon, Dr. Henry Bugbee, to relieve the problem.

The operation must have revealed the prognosis for recovery of his health to be poor. None other than Dr. Truesdale then traveled to Qui-si-Sana late in April. The special railroad sleeping and lounge car once owned by Frank Woolworth was dispatched to pick them up and bring Charlton to Fall River, to the Truesdale Hospital. Dr. Truesdale's own report tells the rest of the story:

> During the early summer it was our privilege to admit as a patient Mr. Earle P. Charlton, President of our Board of Trustees. He was transferred in a private car of the Woolworth Company from his winter home in Palm Beach directly to this hospital. During his stay of six weeks, he made substantial gain in the face of a steadily progressing neoplastic disease.[1] He returned to his summer home, "Pond Meadow" at Westport Harbor, June 10. He shared in the social activities of the summer folks. Summer time, seashore and sunshine ameliorated his suffering and helped stem the outgoing tide of life to some extent.

---

[1] A medical term then in use to denote cancer.

In his power yacht, the Edamena IV, he cruised to nearby ports and to the trial races of the international cup defenders. They sailed a triangular course off Brenton Reef's lightship, Newport, Rhode Island, in August. He witnessed the international cup races over the same course in September. Yachting was Mr. Charlton's favorite outdoor occupation.

He always had a loyal crew and the perfect boat. His requirements were high, but he always found men to meet his standards and they always appeared to enjoy doing it. His pride in the outfit was always apparent. As host he had no peer on land or sea. His less important or more humble guest was given the best he had. I know this from experience.

Thus, the summer was providential. Remote from the cares of business, Mr. Charlton was surrounded by family and friends. The genuine sympathy and wholesome solicitude that he could read in the countenances of his neighborhood callers kept his hope aloft and softened the many hard spots of his physical failures. As if the heavens wanted to help, there were more pleasant sunny days in the summer of 1930 than had been known along the New England coast in many years. On one occasion, he stated that the summer had been the most enjoyable of any in his experience. As the arc of the sun became shorter, the high winds, falling temperature, and rainy days kept him indoors. He failed rapidly and departed this life on November 22 [i.e., 20].[2]

Dr. Truesdale then went on to pay him a finer tribute from long firsthand acquaintance than anyone could possibly pen who studies his life only from written materials:

It seems appropriate here for us to make reference to the high purpose of his benefactions to this institution, wherein his heart had been touched with both joy and sorrow. His own travels, investigations, and experience were sufficient to give him rank among authorities on hospital administration. He understood far better than most persons. He was forgiving, tolerant, and sensitive to the needs of the sick and fallen. Mr. Charlton gave large sums for the development of the physical plant of this institution, but more than this he contributed his time and thought, interest, and advice to enrich the service within the walls of our buildings.

The true source of Mr. Charlton's greatness was his courage, loyalty, and benevolence. These represent the charm which bound the hearts of his associates to him in ties so strong.

---

[2] During his final summer, Charlton received numerous "get well" notes from those unaware of his true condition, as he possibly was himself. Among them was one dated 5 September 1930, from the Coolidges.

He possessed a heart free from all guile and every inordinate selfish feeling. For a man of his resources he practiced self-denial to a degree which became an outstanding virtue. He possessed an uncommon share of diffidence, that quality so rare in little minds but seldom wanting in great ones. Mr. Charlton was offered many important appointments, but it required some degree of finesse to induce him to accept any office. Yet he was never idle. With all these noble talents, the grim messenger of death has swept them from our reach, yet his virtues shall remain engraven on our hearts.

Earle Perry Charlton passed away on 20 November 1930, and was mourned by his many friends, business associates, colleagues, staff, and family. He was buried at the Charlton family mausoleum in the Oak Grove Cemetery in Fall River, Massachusetts.

In *Twenty-Five Years of Progress: 1905–6 – 1930–31* (1931), a history of Truesdale Hospital, Dr. P. E. Truesdale, writes about Charlton after his death:

Recently it was necessary for us to record the death of our outstanding benefactor, Mr. Earle P. Charlton. He was President of our Board of Trustees, a staunch friend and quick to sense our needs. Under his guidance and with his contributions the entire hospital was reconstructed in 1926 and 1927. He gave liberally to complete and equip the south wing. A surgery and laboratory building planned by Mr. E. I. Marvell was added on the north side to complete the original design. For this purpose Mr. Charlton appropriated a sum of $500,000.

It is somewhat difficult to state the exact period when Mr. Charlton centered his attention on this hospital. It is known that medicine, its science and practice, had aroused his interest and won affection early in his life. In 1906 his son Perry was admitted to the Winter Street building as a patient. He had a perforation of the appendix with a spreading peritonitis. At this time Mr. and Mrs. Charlton were in San Francisco. [This was several weeks before the earthquake and fire literally destroyed the city in 1906.] They telephoned instructions and began the journey. The youth recovered after operation. A somewhat perilous situation was averted, for in 1907 the mortality after operations for appendicitis with rupture was very high.

If Mr. Charlton's interest in the hospital was of more than a passing nature after this experience, it was not apparent. Yet it was one of his fine traits of character that he never forgot a genuine kindness. Persons had been known to be rewarded by him weeks, months, or years after rendering him a service even of minor nature. So his impression of 1907 lasted. He traveled extensively over the country, and we saw him only at rare intervals. It was not until after the

War that he became manifestly interested in our organization and in the hospital in which it conducted its activities. His visits were always inspiring because he had a fund of knowledge concerning buildings, business, and administration. No detail of need or waste escaped his discerning observation. He was deeply affected by the sight or even the knowledge of suffering. His greatest happiness appeared to be found in doing something to mitigate the woes of mankind. For example, when the type of elevator was to be signed for in his new surgery, he had installed an extra equipment, a microlevelling devise so that the floor on the elevator would always stop flush with the landing floor. He wished to eliminate any jar to the patients when they were being taken on and off the elevator, even though it meant an added cost of $2,500 to secure this special improvement in the mechanism. In such expressions of thoughtfulness he was without a peer.

When the Board of Directors of the F. W. Woolworth Company learned of Charlton's passing, they issued the following resolution, hand-lettered on vellum and bound in an elegant Morocco leather binding:

At a regular meeting of the Board of Directors of F. W. Woolworth Co. held December tenth, one thousand nine hundred and thirty, the following Resolution was unanimously adopted:

We have learned with profound sorrow of the death of our associate and Vice President, Earle Perry Charlton on November 20th, 1930.

Mr. Charlton was born in Chester, Connecticut, June 19th, 1863. At the age of seventeen he entered the employ of T. C. Newell & Co. of Boston, as salesman. Nine years later, in partnership with Seymour H. Knox, he entered the five and ten cent field, and opened the first store of its kind in Fall River, Massachusetts, which city became his home.

Subsequently the partnership with Mr. Knox was dissolved and Mr. Charlton became the head of an independent chain of five and ten cent stores, becoming pioneer in opening stores of this class west of the Rocky Mountains. In 1912 he become one of the founders of F. W. Woolworth Co.

This briefly, is the business record of Earle Perry Charlton, but we take pride also in the positions of honor and trust which he filled with distinction and faithfulness. Public institutions were greatly benefited by his generosity and through his interest and painstaking service.

It is, however, to the more intimate qualities of heart and mind that we wish to pay tribute. Loyalty to his friends and to this company was his outstanding characteristic. Added to this was a fine sense of justice, a conscientious fidelity to duty, a high-mindedness in all his dealings, and a vital sympathy toward his associates, that endeared him to us all.

This company has lost an able officer and Director, and we a warm personal friend.

Resolved, that this tribute of respect be spread in full on the minutes of this meeting and that a suitably engrossed copy, signed by the Chairman of this Board and the President of the Company, attested the Secretary, be presented to Mrs. Charlton as an expression of our deep sympathy in her loss.

Signed

C. S. Woolworth
Chairman of the Board

In his last will and testament (see Documentary appendix, 46), Charlton divided his estate with discernment among family, friends, and above all saw to it that his charitable impulses would be imbued with permanency. The following chapter will examine the continuing mission of the Charlton Foundation he created, but in closing, it will be sufficient here to note how he treated his family and loyal retainers, and perhaps more importantly, the basis of the philanthropic trusts he created.

Named as his executors were the First National Bank of Boston, his wife Ida Stein Charlton, and his daughter Virginia Charlton Lincoln. Ida was given outright all of his liquid assets, as well as all of his domestic real estate. Each of his children were left the sum of $100,000, while his grandchildren each received $25,000, as did his secretary, Mary A. Dunne. His siblings, John Howard Charlton and Mary Charlton Bardol, as well as his brother-in-law, Dr. Ulysses B. Stein, each received $25,000. Three nieces and a nephew each received $10,000.

Among "loyal and efficient domestic help," his former chauffeur George F. Donnelly received $10,000, while the staff at Pond Meadow—Anna McGillivray, Louise Carlson, Anna McDonough, Louis Perini, and George Cook—were each granted $5,000. There were also several bequests of $1,000 to staff at the Quequechan Club in Fall River.

But the bulk of Earle Charlton's assets was otherwise divided into two sections, the Charlton Charity Trust and the Charlton Building Trust, and these consisted, respectively, of 10,000 shares of Woolworth capital stock and parcels of land he had acquired in and around Fall River. Of the Woolworth stock in the Charlton Charity Trust, a quarter, valued at not less than $500,000, was reserved for the Truesdale Hospital. The residue was to be divided into two funds, the E. P. Charlton Fund, one third of whose income was to go for medical research and medical fellowships at Tufts University, while half of the remaining income was to be designated the Ida S. Charlton Fund and given to the Union Hospital of Fall River.

The Charlton Building Trust was to consist of all real estate holdings, plus 20,000 shares of Woolworth stock, the income of which was reserved for Ida S. Charlton during her lifetime, and after her death divided between her three children. It was stipulated that, insofar as feasible, reinvestments, if any, were to be made in Woolworth stock.

Charlton's sweet success during his lifetime seems unique in two aspects. The first is that all his money was earned honorably and without hindrance to others, and the second that his impulse to alleviate the suffering of others ran so deep. Of men like Andrew Carnegie, John D. Rockefeller, it might be said that they both possessed and gave away more money than Earle Charlton, but it cannot be claimed that they gave away more in proportion to their holdings than he, or that they had garnered their wealth with honestly and sensitivity. Still other multimillionaires, like John Jacob Astor (who hardly amassed all his money honorably) and indeed Frank Winfield Woolworth himself (who did), were relatively untouched by any charitable impulses at all.

Perhaps herein lies the measure of Earle P. Charlton: his good fortune became the good fortune of humanity. And along the way, there was no man who did not admire and respect, even love, him.

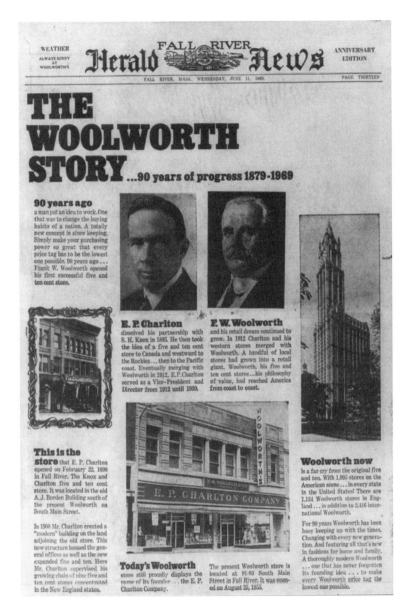

Fig. 22. Fall River has long been appreciative of E. P. Charlton's accomplishments and on June 11, 1969, the Fall River *Herald News* issued a special anniversary edition celebrating Charlton and the Woolworth Company. Reproduced with permission of the Fall River *Herald News*.

VII

THE LASTING LEGACY

EARLE PERRY CHARLTON believed fervently that good health was the cornerstone to a productive and happy existence, and through creation of the Charlton Charitable Trusts he was able to assure after his death that his lifelong desire to help people and alleviate their suffering would continue indefinitely. Even today, his benevolence benefits thousands, yet unborn in 1930, through provision of facilities for hospital care, new procedures, medical research and medical education.

SETTING UP CHARITABLE TRUSTS

One of the great legacies that Charlton left when he died in 1930, at the comparatively young age of 67, was that he had the incredible foresight to set up numerous charitable trusts with the advice and counsel of the First National Bank of Boston, for which he was a director. He left specific instructions on how the trusts were to be administered and who was to receive the benefit of them. Additional charitable trusts were set within three years of his death in the name of his wife Ida and his children, with the assistance of the First National Bank, which became co-trustee of all of the trusts.

Putting money aside for charitable purposes even during their lifetimes was not characteristic of many of the great American merchant families. As it turned out, however, this was not true for four of the five founders of the Woolworth Co. Fred Kirby, of Wilkes-Barre, Penn., was a major contributor to many philanthropic projects throughout his life, which continues with the Kirby Foundation. Seymour Knox was an active philanthropist in his birthplace of Russell, N.Y., and Sumner Woolworth was also an active philanthropist during his lifetime.

Only Frank Woolworth declined to use his vast fortune to any great extent in the field of philanthropy. As remarked earlier, he was overly frugal with his fortune, doling out cash on the barrelhead for everything from his stately homes in New York and Long Island to the construction of the great 60-story Woolworth Building in lower Manhattan, paying its costs floor-by-floor to the tune of $13,500,000 by the time it opened in April 1913.

Woolworth left virtually his entire fortune to his family, and a major part of it eventually ended up with Barbara Hutton, his granddaughter. Throughout her life, she was often portrayed as "The Million Dollar Baby," "Poor Little Rich Girl," and "Babs," three titles that she detested. In spite of all her wealth, she was not able to enjoy her life, as she invariably would end up in the company of men who were more interested in her vast wealth rather than her. She was a very generous person and felt as though she had to pay for friendships in order to keep them. After paying exorbitant alimony to six of her seven husbands (Cary Grant was the only one who would not take her money),[1] and being characterized as "one of the most lavish spenders of all time,"[2] she managed to go through an estimated fortune of $50,000,000! Barbara died on 11 May 1979 at the age of 66, a lonely recluse and virtually penniless.

THE LEGACY BEGINS

When Charlton died he left an estate of $32,000,000, with over $2,900,000 earmarked for charity, besides having already given away at least half that much during his lifetime. His was easily the largest estate ever left by a Fall River resident. In Fall River alone, Charlton bequeathed generous endowments to the Truesdale Hospital, the District

---

[1] Barbara Hutton was married to her second husband, Count Haugvntz-Reventlow, at the home of Dr. and Mrs. A. J. (Bart) Hood in Reno, Nevada, on 13 May 1935. Mrs. Hood was the former wife of Earle Perry Charlton, Jr., and both her daughter Thelma and son Earle P. Charlton II were present at the wedding.

[2] See Dean Jennings, *Barbara Hutton: A Candid Biography* (New York: Frederick Fell, 1968).

Nursing Association, the Central Congregational Church, the Boys' Club, the YMCA, the Home for the Aged, the Children's Home, St. Vincent's Orphan Home, the Ninth Street Nursery, and the St. John's Day Nursery. During the 1920s, as has already been noted, he had funded a new addition to the Truesdale Hospital in Fall River, which included a complete new surgery wing; the cost: a half-million dollars, in a currency then very much harder than ours today.

CHARLTON MEMORIAL HOSPITAL

For nearly fifty years after Charlton's death, the trustees of the Charlton Charitable Trusts, which included his eldest daughter, Ruth Charlton Mitchell Masson, and the First National Bank of Boston, managed the funds that had been set up before and after his death. Then, in 1979, an opportunity arose that seemed the perfect expression of the founder's will, a project that would be medically related and one that would benefit his beloved city of Fall River.

Fall River had been through two dramatic changes in the past century that changed both its purpose for existence and its capacity for continuing to be a viable community. During the 1800s Fall River was one of the major fishing ports in New England for supplying the region with a multitude of fish and seafood. Fishermen from Portugal migrated there, to establish their roots and raise their families. When, in the course of time, the fishing industry largely moved elsewhere, the city looked for another industry to take its place. In the late 1800s, textile mill operators were searching for locations that had an abundance of waterpower and available manpower to operate new textile mills, and Fall River (along with New Bedford) filled their needs perfectly. Subsequently, the growth of its textile manufactures made Fall River one of the nation's largest and most important producers of cotton products. Clearly, the city had entered a period of prosperity and many fortunes were made during this very productive era. Unfortunately after World War I, in the middle 1920s after a spate of labor troubles in New England, the mills started to move southward, to below the Mason-Dixon line, where cheaper, and non-unionized labor was available. This eventually left Fall River without a major industry, and made it difficult to support its three major health care facilities.

The population of Fall River was predominately Catholic, and its St. Anne's Hospital took care of a large portion of the city's Portuguese population. By the 1970s this left the Truesdale and the Union Hospitals, both strong influences within the city, competing for a diminishing clientele and patronage, while neither of their administrators or medical staffs wished to forgo their independence. If there was any chance of merging the two hospitals into one, a new name would have to be found, and it was agreed by all that the Charlton name would have instant recognition and widespread approval from the community. Hence it was that both Truesdale and Union Hospitals began to negotiate with the Charlton family, namely Ruth Charlton Mitchell Masson, and the family's private banker at the First National Bank of Boston, Waldo E. Dodge.

Frederic C. Dreyer, Jr., administrator and CEO of Charlton Memorial Hospital, and the Rev. Dr. Robert P. Lawrence, director of development, were the main principals in convincing Ruth Masson, who now lived in Rochester, Minn., that this would be a wonderful opportunity to name the new merged hospitals after her father Earle Perry Charlton.

> Dreyer gives credit to Rev. Dr. Lawrence for playing the central role in the rapprochement which resulted in a $1 million contribution to the building fund and renaming of Union-Truesdale to Charlton Memorial Hospital Dreyer and Rev. Dr. Lawrence made several trips to Rochester to reestablish links with Mrs. Masson, then in her late eighties, and update her on hospital progress. On behalf of the hospital board, Donald Ramsbottom also established rapport with Mrs. Masson and paid a visit. With utmost skill and diplomacy, he delineated the volunteer dimension of the hospital and system.[3]

It was finally agreed that the new hospital would receive $1,000,000 from the Charlton Charitable Trusts and that they should merge to become the Charlton Memorial Hospital, on 1 March 1980.[4]

---

[3] See David M. Eskes, Earle P. Charlton II, Fred C. Dreyer, Jr., and Rev. Dr. Robert P. Lawrence, *Our Story: Charlton Health System* (Phoenix: Heritage Publishers, 1997).

[4] The principals in this merger were Ruth Charlton Mitchell Masson, Waldo E. Dodge of the First National Bank of Boston, and the trustees of the Charlton Charitable Trusts: John F. Dator, chairman of Union-Truesdale Hospital (1978–80), Donald H. Ramsbottom, chairman of Charlton Memorial Hospital (1980–85), Frederic C. Dreyer, Jr., administrator and CEO of Charlton Memorial Hospital, and the Rev. Dr. Robert P. Lawrence, director of development for the hospital. Members of the Charlton family in attendance for the merger ceremonies included Mr. and Mrs. E. P. Charlton II and their

With the two hospitals merging, a plan was developing to add a new five story, 156,724- square-foot tower to the hospital, which was located at the Union Hospital site on historic Highland Avenue. The new tower would be a state-of-the-art complex that featured 192 single-patient rooms, new emergency, radiology, and outpatient departments, and intensive- and progressive-care units. Provision for a future M.R.I. unit, a helicopter pad, and a new parking garage were to follow. The new tower would be dedicated in the memory of Dr. Warren G. Atwood, a well known and respected Fall River physician who was president of Truesdale Hospital from 1943 to 1946.

On 27 May 1983 the 344-bed Charlton Memorial Hospital, with the newly constructed 192-bed Atwood Tower, was officially dedicated with Margaret Heckler, Secretary of HEW, from Washington, State Senator Mary Fonseca, and State Rep. Joan Menard on the speakers' program, along with local dignitaries and Charlton Memorial Hospital officials. Ruth Charlton Mitchell Masson could not make the trip from Rochester, but her nephew Earle P. Charlton II attended and spoke for the Charlton family. Subsequently, in future years, Charlton Memorial received three additional trusts—two from the E. P. Charlton estate, and another in the form of a bequest from Ruth Charlton Mitchell Masson.

RUTH CHARLTON MITCHELL MASSON AND THE MAYO CLINIC

In March 1960 Ruth Mitchell's first husband, Frederick Mitchell, died after a long illness, and five years later in 1965, she married Dr. James C. Masson, a noted physician at the Mayo Clinic and an old family friend. She then moved to Rochester, Minn., where she became acquainted with the eminent physicians of that famous institution. Dr. Masson himself died in 1972, and from 1973 Mrs. Masson directed much of her philanthropy toward the Mayo Clinic as the principal trustee of the Charlton Charitable Trusts. From 1973 to 1989 she made six major contributions to the clinic and its medical school as follows.

---

daughter Stacey, and Col. and Mrs. Fraser E. West (Thelma Charlton) and daughter Karen.

1973. The James C. Masson Professorship of Surgery was established to recognize a Mayo surgeon's academic contributions to surgery.

1976. The Frederick M. Mitchell Scholarship was created to award student merit scholarships at the Mayo Medical School.

1978. Charlton Hall, in the Guggenheim Building, was established as the primary lecture hall at the Mayo Medical School.

1984. The Ruth and Frederick Mitchell Research Trust was founded as an endowment for research at the Mayo Clinic for cancer and other diseases.

1984. The Ruth and Frederick Mitchell Student Center, formerly the Rochester Public Library, was rebuilt for use by the Mayo Medical School.

1989. The Charlton Building at the Mayo Clinic, 200,000 square feet, houses one of the world's largest cancer radiation centers and includes a unit devoted to transfusion medicine, a pain clinic, a nuclear medicine unit, a diagnostic radiology unit, and an obstetrics unit. The cost of the building was $35,000,000. Subsequently, five additional floors were added in 1999.

After Ruth Charlton Mitchell Masson's death in 1995 at the age of 104, 80% of her estate went to the Mayo Clinic,[5] and the remaining 20% was placed into another trust for the benefit of the Charlton Memorial Hospital in Fall River. Meanwhile, the Charlton Memorial Hospital had received the three trusts already mentioned, one to each institution as provided in Earle Charlton's will and a third upon their merger in 1980. It now benefits from all four Charlton trusts.

In 1983, Earle P. Charlton II was named as a trustee and joined Ruth Charlton Mitchell Masson, Waldo E. Dodge, Alfred W. Fuller, and the First National Bank of Boston in that capacity. Even before Mrs. Masson's death the focus of the Charlton Charitable Trusts by common consent had shifted back to Massachusetts, where Earle Charlton had intended his charitable bequests to be centered, especially Fall River, Boston, and southeastern Massachusetts. His grandson, E. P. Charlton II, and the other trustees felt that most future grants should be made there, an area where Earle Charlton had worked, lived, and loved, and where his contributions "could really make a difference."

---

[5] The 80% of the estate was divided as follows: the Mayo Clinic Foundation received 70%, and the Rochester Methodist Hospital and St. Mary's Hospital (Mayo affiliates) each received 5%.

Accordingly, beginning in 1985, the Charlton Charitable Trusts made strong commitments to a range of projects that included the refurbishment of charitable institutions in the Fall River area, to hospital initiatives both in Fall River and in Boston, a chair at Harvard for physical medicine and rehabilitation, and, finally, to a new business college at the University of Massachusetts Dartmouth. The projects were dedicated to Earle Perry Charlton, Earle and Ida Charlton, Ruth Charlton Mitchell, and Virginia Charlton Lincoln. Following is a listing of these major projects and grants.

1989. The Family Service Agency building, the Charlton Building, was established in Fall River.

1989. The Earle P. and Ida S. Charlton Building was dedicated by the United Way of Greater Fall River.

1989. The E. P. Charlton, Jr. Trust Wing was founded in Ellison 6, Orthopedics Wing, Massachusetts General Hospital, Boston. (The Charlton Trusts also underwrites diabetic research at this hospital.)

1991. The Virginia C. Lincoln Center for Women, at the Charlton Memorial Hospital, Fall River.

1992. The Ruth Charlton Mitchell Therapies Center, located on the campus of Charlton Memorial Hospital, Fall River.

1996. The Earle P. and Ida S. Charlton Professorship was the first endowed chair at the Spaulding Rehabilitation Hospital in Boston and the first Harvard Chair in Physical Education and Rehabilitation; the grant totaled $2,750,000 for the Harvard Chair.

1996. The Earle P. Charlton College of Business and Industry was endowed at University of Massachusetts Dartmouth, the only four-year university in southeastern Massachusetts. This $3,000,000 grant was the largest ever received by the institution, or by any public university in the Commonwealth.

In addition to the large grants listed above, the Charlton Charitable Trusts continue to support local charities in the Fall River and Boston areas. Included are the United Way of Greater Fall River, the Boys' and Girls' Club of Fall River, the Family Service Agency of Greater Fall River, the Clarke School for the Deaf, the Forsyth Dental Center in Boston, the Red Cross, the American Cancer Society, the Y.M.C.A. of

Greater Fall River, the Fall River Historical Society, the Diabetes Foundation of Greater Fall River, and diabetes research at the Massachusetts General Hospital, Boston, and many others.

None of the philanthropic activities listed above would have been possible were it not for the forward thinking and regard for human needs that long ago existed in the mind of Earle Charlton, the son of an artisan who earned his fortune by hard work, and a scrupulous attention to detail. Seventy years after his death, still faithful to his wishes, his legacy continues and is likely to continue for generations to come.

AN UNEXPECTED BOON

There is a footnote to this chapter on the charitable legacy of Charlton. In his final year, he had the foresight to create numerous charitable trusts within his will, each containing instructions on how they must be administered and who was to receive their benefits. For example, it has been mentioned that as a trustee of Tufts University, he created the sizeable educational fund for its medical college, which still exists and is still educating medical fellows. But at least one of his charities, in fact not included in his last will and testament and dating from 1921, has surfaced only recently and has assumed a form he never could have envisioned.

In that year, he gave 25 shares of Woolworth stock to Mr. Broomhead, then head of the Bradford Durfee Textile School in Fall River, for fellowships to "Young men born in the city of Fall River" who were interested in that trade. Awards to students were to be limited to $200 per year. But interest in the textile industry declined, and the stock was put into the B. M. C. Durfee Trust and literally forgotten for the next sixty years. During this time, the Bradford Durfee School became Southeastern Massachusetts Technological Institute (1964–69) and later moved to North Dartmouth, where it became Southeastern Massachusetts University (1969–91), and finally the University of Massachusetts Dartmouth, in 1991.

During one of the audits—which took place when the bank changed ownership—the 25 shares of Woolworth stock were uncovered and brought to the attention of the University. It developed that the shares were now worth $80,000! In 1989, the stock was put into a merit scholarship at the University of Massachusetts, Dartmouth, whereupon the trustees of the Charlton Charitable Trusts added an extra $20,000 to make the scholarship endowment worth a total of $100,000. The fund now rewards up to seven students with stipends of up to $1000 per year.

EPILOGUE
THE END OF AN ERA

ON JULY 17, 1997 it was announced that the remaining 400 Woolworth stores in the United States were to be closed, ending 118 years of Woolworth store operation. It was not merely an economic event. It was a way of life gone, and to those beyond middle age it dramatized (as the demise of no other commercial institution could) that management's search for increased profits were to be made at the expense of tradition and service. Gone were the familiar gold letters on the red storefronts, the plain wooden floorboards, the smell of popcorn popping and the individual cash registers ringing at each individual counter which for almost a century identified an institution which had served an infinite variety of needs.

Woolworth's had been the unique place in any downtown where one could repair in the certainty of finding a gallimaufry of necessities such as Scotch tape, ball point pens, thread, zippers, jam, Cutex nail polish, Ponds Cold Cream, Jergens Lotion, "Evening in Paris" perfume, Mabelline eye shadow, Hula Hoops, Mickey Mouse balloons, Fruit of the Loom underwear, Herald Square stationery, hair nets, toothbrushes, Aqua Net hair spray, brassieres, nylons, Elmer's white glue, nightlights, inexpensive dinnerware, paper plates, stainless steel flatware, pots and pans, tools, hardware and the largest candy counter in town where you could buy a nickel's worth of gum drops or a dime's worth of peanut clusters.

And who could forget the Woolworth soda fountains, or lunch counters where people could find their "cokes," creamy ice cream sodas, "tulip" sundaes, and economical meals such as a green beans, meatloaf-and-gravy or hot turkey dinner or just an old fashioned BLT (bacon lettuce and tomato sandwich). It was the place to visit and meet your friends. Occasionally, you would hear salesladies in their house dresses or smocks call a customer "honey" or "sweetie." As one boutique manager complained, "Where do I send my girls now, when I need a box of pins or some blue crepe paper?"

Woolworth's had been a mainstay in England too, and the *International Herald-Tribune,* of 21 November 1997 carried a letter from one irate reader when the news was announced: "Is nothing sacred? I depended upon Woolworth's and so did my friends...." Luckily for him, his implied prayer was answered: instead of closing forever, the United Kingdom stores and their contents did not cease to exist, for they had previously been sold to the English Kingfisher company, which has maintained almost all the stores and preserved the Woolworth name and logo. Thus, they sail profitably on, while Woolworth stores in the United States and Canada are only a memory.

GOING, GOING, GONE!

To better understand what happened to the Woolworth chain of stores, one has to look at the changes that were being made by the retailing industry after World War 11. Chains were going in different directions and diversifying their stores and merchandise mix. Variety stores were being upstaged by new type stores such as K-Mart (a division of S. S. Kresge), discount drug stores, and factory outlets which started up in the abandoned mills in New England. In order to compete with these stores and diversify, Woolworth made a big—and disastrous—decision. After finally attaining annual sales of one billion dollars in 1960, the company opened their first Woolco stores in the United States and Canada in 1962. These stores were meant to compete with K-Marts and other fledging discount stores that were springing up all over the countryside, but they were never a factor against their competition and the company ended up closing the entire U.S. chain in 1982. The Woolco stores in Canada fared considerably better and lasted until 1994 when they were sold to the Canadian Wal-Mart. In 1982 Woolworth also sold its 52.6 per cent interest in Woolworth Ltd., its British Company, to Kingfisher. The English chain was still very profitable, but the company needed the additional money that they received from the sale of the English company to finance their new operations in the United States.

In 1965, Woolworth acquired the G. R. Kinney Corporation which was the nation's oldest and largest shoe chain. It was a conservative ladies and mens shoe store chain that eventually was changed to a format featuring casual and sports shoes. The company augmented its Kinney Stores with Foot Locker, Lady Foot Locker, Kids Foot Locker, Footquarters, and Athletic X-Press Stores, most of which were an immediate success. In 1969 Woolworth acquired the Richmond Brothers Company, a manufacturer of mens and boys clothing, along with an established chain of retail outlets, but it, along with Anderson-Little mens and ladies apparel stores, did not do well and the company ended up selling both chains in 1991 and 1992.

Other chain stores that Woolworth opened or purchased in the 60s, 70s, and 80s included *J. Brannam, an off-price brand-name clothing and footwear retail chain, Kids Mart, Susie's, Shirt Closet, Final Cut, Little Folk Shop, Sportelle, Herald Square Party Shop, The Best of Times, Randy River, The Rx Place, Going to the Game, Woolworth Express, and Woolworth Garden Centers. All of these chains were either closed, or sold to other companies.

Meanwhile sales and profits in the original Woolworth stores in the United States had been declining each year. Sales for the entire company in 1996, the last complete year of operation, were $8.1 billion, and of that total, the Woolworth stores represented less than $2.9 billion. Total operating loss for Woolworth stores for 1996 was 36 million dollars. This is not surprising as the company was using what profit they were getting from the Woolworth stores to promote newer store formats, particularly Woolco and *J. Brannam. Instead of upgrading and finding better locations for the existing Woolworth stores and trying to put additional lines like pharmacies, into the Woolworth stores, they poured the profits into new concept stores that were eventually to end up as financial losses.

In 1993 the Executive Office announced that they were going to close "about" 400 of the remaining 1,465 Woolworth stores, followed by announcements that 1,000 more stores would be closed or converted to other formats in 1995 and 1996. They actually closed around 665 stores and then, on July 17, 1997, the Chairman of the Board, Roger Farah, announced that the Woolworth Company would be closing the remaining 400 Woolworth stores in the United States and that the Woolworth format would cease to exist.[1] Over 9,200 employees would be terminated or re-located in other stores.[2]

Thus ended not only an era of retailing, but an epoch of social history. In America and Canada, through Depression, hard times, and war, the stores had nurtured all classes from socialites to down-and-outers, and to juveniles in search of an ice cream cone or a toy fire engine. Wherever one encountered the gold-on-red letters far from home, they were a point of reference, a convenience, and a comfort.

By 1997, most of the old name 5 & 10s or variety stores that had competed with Woolworth for over a decade had vanished. Gone were the old storefronts of S. S. Kresge, S. H. Kress, J. J. Newberry, J. G. McCrory, and W. T. Grant. Kresge had become K-Mart, but the rest had disappeared from the retail field and Woolworth had become part of an extinct brand of retailers. It would seem that the variety stores as a whole no longer generated sufficient sales to attract shoppers, while the newer, high-volume drug stores in shopping malls with their prescription departments (and in many states, high-volume liquor sales) in part filled the void they left by furnishing many, but not all, of the same items.

Perhaps even more than the drugstore chains, the "big box" stores like K-Mart, Wal-Mart, and Target are the true offspring of the varieties, though on a far less human scale. Woolworth occupied strategic downtown real estate and represented human dimensions, while these megastores are isolated in the midst of suburban parking lots that dwarf football fields. Inside, aisles stretch to the horizons and induce reactions such as, "now that I'm here, who is going to help me find what I came there for?" Founded upon the concept of "one-stop shopping," they are unreachable without recourse to the automobile and items like laundry bags or shoe brushes are virtually unfindable without the help of personnel involved in provisioning aisles—who must spend a good part of their working days directing people.

One might even believe that the "one-stop" concept is in fact the antithesis of those social values typifying the old variety store. One never

---

[1] There is also a Woolworth in Australia, but the name exists only because the parent company neglected to register the name in that country and enterprising entrepreneurs took the name and started their own company.

[2] After all of the Woolworth stores in the United States were closed, the new company (the Venator Group) closed or sold the remainder of the Woolworth stores in Canada, Mexico, Spain and Germany.

encounters the same employee twice, elderly salesladies with dyed hair have vanished along with the counters they served, and everything smaller than a basketball is wrapped in plastic and stuck to a card so that it can be hung on a hook. To inspect something at close hand, you have to buy it and tear open the package.

Obviously, times and patterns have changed. In some cities, downtowns were monumentalized to the point where people no longer went there to shop for daily needs (witness St. Louis and Detroit). In others, like Minneapolis, the Woolworth stores were stranded in decaying districts whose best days lay behind; spaces where buildings had been demolished became parking lots and the stores shared blocks with "adult" bookstores and over-the-hill-saloons. Healthy downtowns survive mostly in cities like Boston, Chicago, Providence, New York, and San Francisco where office buildings and public transport create dense concentrations of population. Where downtowns survive and even thrive, variety stores did well and would still profitably serve the needs of their traditional clientele. The boutique manager "in heavily-touristed Charleston said it all in her reaction to the Lady Foot Locker store which opened on Woolworth's prime King Street site: "It almost makes me sick whenever I notice the old diamonds with the Ws still visible above the new facade! Tennis shoes, my foot!"

At the Woolworth's Stockholder Meeting on June 11, 1998, at the Arsenal Mall in Watertown, Massachusetts, Roger N. Farah, CEO, announced that as of June 12, 1998 the Woolworth Company name would be changed to the Venator Group. The company felt that the name, which means "sportsman" in Latin, identifies with the merchandise that the company will be selling in the future.[3]

Several weeks after the stockholders meeting, it was announced that the new Venator Group would sell the 60 story Woolworth Building in New York City for "about $155 million" and that they would move their offices to another building in New York City.

The remaining stores that would be operated by The Venator Group include the shoe store chain (ex Kinney) which is now called Global Athletic Group and contains Foot Locker, Ladies Foot Locker, Kids Foot Locker, and Champs Sports. Other stores include the Northern Group of

---

[3] There were two protests from the floor of the meeting, one from E. P. Charlton II, and one from the Greenway Partners L. P., a New York investment group with a 6.1 per cent stake in Woolworth's. Though their protests were heard, they had no effect.

stores: Northern Reflections, Northern Getaway, and Northern Elements. The companies remaining businesses include Afterthoughts, which is a Jewelry format and the San Francisco Music Box and Gift Company.

WHAT HAPPENED?

Why did what was once "America's Store" fail after so many productive years? The answers are complex, but it is clear that the variety store concept no longer represented a profitable type of operation that could generate enough sales to make it a viable format for future retailing. Although it was only a matter of time before the demise of the Woolworth stores, there are many who believe that Woolworth could have emerged from its eventual downward spiral by changing its image, taking on new high volume departments such as pharmacies and liquor, and patterning themselves after successful drug chains such as Walgreens.

The reasons why the Woolworth stores did not survive the 20th Century can be summarized in several points.

1. The existing Woolworth stores were not in tune with the merchandising that was being exhibited by the new-look stores (e.g., Wall Mart or Office Depot) and a multitude of other stores who carried identical merchandise (e.g., convenience stores, supermarkets, and drug stores).

2. Many of the largest Woolworth stores were located in old downtown areas that were no longer viable shopping locations. The large area shopping centers had changed the pattern of shopping and consumers were going elsewhere.

3. One aspect that had been very favorable for Woolworth for many years turned sour. The 50-year and 100-year leases that Mr. Woolworth and the other founders had set up at very low rent figures were either starting to run out or were keeping the stores from moving to more desirable shopping-center locations. In many cases, the rents in the major shopping centers were far too high.

4. The Woolworth buyers should have been more creative in the merchandise mix that they put into the stores. The average sale per foot was very low in the stores, and regional merchandising was not popular with the buyers. The advantage of regional buying was proved in Hawaii where the district manager and his store managers were given more leeway in the merchandising of their stores, and they became the largest sales and profit stores in the company.

5. As for improving the merchandise mix, the Executive Office should have been bolder in placing high volume and high gross departments such as pharmacies in most all stores. The profits from the prescription drugs would have paid the rent and more. Likewise, liquor departments should have been placed in selected stores to increase the sales volume. This was done with great success by many of the large drugstore chains.

It is hardly satisfactory to moralize on the ethos surrounding management's decision to terminate what had once been a thriving and useful institution; to do so would only be another lament to the tune of "O tempora, O mores." It can never be known if E. P. Charlton would have voted with the nay-sayers who recently closed the Woolworth stores; perhaps he would have, purely on the ground of pragmatism. Then again, many businessmen of his generation tempered the pure profit motive with human concern and tended to be mindful of those dependent on them. Certainly, as one can see from the foregoing chapters, Charlton lacked neither public spirit nor feeling for his customers. Moreover, he illustrated that one could build and operate a transcontinental business in an era where the only tools were typewriters, carbon paper, the two-cent letter, and if necessary, a long-distance telephone call, or telegram.

All in all, Charlton was an important player in developing a way of life which perhaps unfortunately has not transcended his times. For during them, the Charlton and Woolworth stores were part of the nation's social fabric (indeed that of four nations) and the role they played was humanizing, constructive, and positive. People met at the luncheon counter, and they came to know and converse with the employees. If away from home, they could easily relate to the familiar scene the Woolworth stores provided. But while the megastores that replaced them are their true offspring, their impersonality and their awesome scale are anything but socially redeeming, and one can never find in them the intimacy and the reassurance of yesteryear's Woolworth chain. We must therefore salute E. P. Charlton—in whose public and personal life we can perceive that kindly spirit of a bygone America so many of us fear we may never find again.

DOCUMENTARY APPENDIX

Primary documents are the lifeblood of history, for historians employ the first-hand facts they embody to write new histories with different, and wider, emphases. It is for this reason that the authors have decided to transcribe and print the entire surviving correspondence between E. P. Charlton and Simon Kapstein. In addition the original contract between S. H. Knox and Charlton has been included, as has the last will and testament of E. P. Charlton. All the letters from Charlton are on official home office letterhead; a few are signed. Most of the letters from Kapstein to Charlton are second copies, unsigned.

Most of these documents are typewritten, but a few are wholly in manuscript (or handwritten). Some typewritten documents have been altered in manuscript (MS). All alterations are indicated in square brackets and the nature of the alteration is indicated in italics. Original spelling, punctuation, and grammar has been retained unaltered.

The letters of E. P. Charlton and E.A. Bardol are printed with permission of E. P. Charlton II. The letters of Simon Kapstein are printed with permission of Robert Kerner.

IMPORTANT DATES

date	event
1863, June 19	Earle Perry Charlton born, Chester, Conn.
1868, Sept. 10	Ida M. Stein born, Buffalo, N.Y.
1889, June 19	Married Ida M. Stein, Buffalo, N.Y.
1889, Dec. 13	Partnership with S. H. Knox
1890, Feb. 22	First Knox & Charlton store opened in Fall River
1891, Jan. 31	Ruth Charlton Mitchell Masson born
1893, Aug. 23	Earle Perry Charlton, Jr., born
1895, May 21	Virginia Charlton Lincoln born
1896, Jan. 1	E. P. Charlton & Co. formed
1907, June 14	E. P. Charlton & Co. incorporated
1908, Feb. 28	New E. P. Charlton store opens in Fall River
1910, Nov. 13	Charlton Mills open in Fall River
1912, Jan. 1	F. W. Woolworth Co. formed; Charlton made Vice President and Director
1914, June 11	Ruth Charlton marries Frederick (Fritz) Mencke Mitchell
1915, April 17	Pond Meadow destroyed by fire
1925	E. P. Charlton becomes president of Truesdale Hospital Board
1930, Nov. 20	E. P. Charlton dies, 67 years old
1957, Aug. 30	Ida S. Charlton dies, 88 years old
1960, March 27	Fredrick M. (Fritz) Mitchell dies, 70 years old
1965, Nov.	Ruth Mitchell marries Dr. James C. Masson
1970, June 13	E. P. Charlton Fall River store closes after 62 years
1972, Dec. 7	Dr. James C. Masson dies, 91 years old
1973, June 7	E. P. Charlton, Jr., dies, 79 years old
1977, Aug. 19–20	Pond Meadow contents auctioned
1980, March 1	Truesdale and Union hospitals merged to become the Charlton Memorial Hospital
1982, Oct. 17	Virginia Charlton Lincoln dies, 87 years old
1995, Feb. 11	Ruth Charlton Mitchell Masson dies, 104 years old

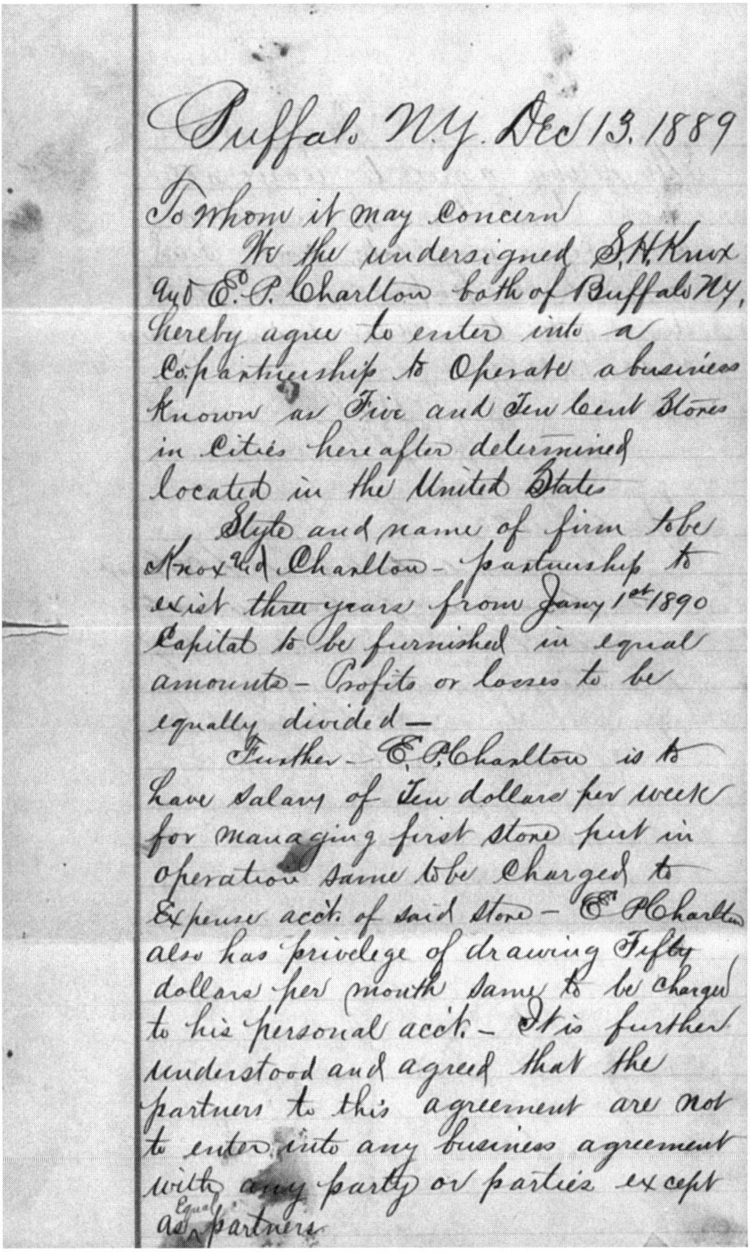

Buffalo N.Y. Dec 13. 1889

To Whom it may Concern

We the undersigned S.H. Knox and E.P. Charlton both of Buffalo N.Y, hereby agree to enter into a Copartnership to Operate a business known as Five and Ten Cent Stores in Cities hereafter determined located in the United States

Style and name of firm to be Knox and Charlton — partnership to exist three years from Jany 1st 1890 Capital to be furnished in equal amounts — Profits or losses to be equally divided —

Further — E.P. Charlton is to have Salary of Ten dollars per week for managing first store put in Operation same to be charged to Expense acct. of said store — E.P. Charlton also has privilege of drawing Fifty dollars per month same to be charged to his personal acct. — It is further understood and agreed that the partners to this agreement are not to enter into any business agreement with any party or parties except as partners

Fig. 23. Document 1, page 1.

1.

[Whole document in MS.]

Buffalo N.Y. Dec 13. 1889

To Whom it may concern

We the undersigned S. H. Knox and E. P. Charlton both of Buffalo N.Y., hereby agree to enter into copartnership to operate a business known as Five and Ten Cent Stores in cities here after determined located in the United States.

Style and name of firm to be Knox and Charlton – partnership to exist three years from Jan 1st 1890 Capital to be furnished in equal amounts – Profits or losses to be equally divided –

Further – E. P. Charlton is to have salary of Ten dollars per week for managing first store put in operation same to be charged to Expense acc't. of said store – E. P. Charlton also has privelege of drawing Fifty dollars per month same to be charged to his personal acc't. – It is further understood and agreed that the partners to this agreement are not to enter into any business agreement with any party or parties except as equal partners.

It is further agreed and understood that S. H. Knox has privelege of conducting business he is now interested in namely with F. W. Woolworth, H. C. Haywood & M. B. McBrier in Erie. Pa. Buffalo, N.Y. Lockport N.Y. and town hereafter decided upon with H C Haywood during the tern of this contract No money $$ to be drawn from firm of Knox & Charlton during the term of this contract but profits to be used in opening new stores as fast as sufficient money is made to open store and pay in any and all cases cash for goods. –

S.H. Knox Further agrees to loan E. P. Charlton if necessary Fifteen hundred dollars and take his note at 6% per annum due on day from date but agrees not to demand payment except in case of death or dissolution until the expiration of this partnership agreement Witness

	S. H. Knox
Ida Stein Charlton	E. P. Charlton
Daisy Burrow	

Dec 17. 1889

We hereby agree to waive all right to indorse personally or as a firm any Note, Draft, Bond or Negotiable paper of any kind during the time named in agreement of Dec 13. 1889.

S. H. Knox

E. P. Charlton

Jan 6th 1890

It is understood that S. H. Knox has privelege of opening a store in Detroit Mich. independent of the terms named in this contract

S. H. Knox

E. P. Charlton

2.

Fall River, Mass.
Feb. 11, 1908

Mr. Simon Kapstein,
c/o E. P. Charlton & Co.,
Portland, Oregon.

My dear Simon:

I am in receipt of yours and note what you have to say in regard to the prospects of Portland. I believe, as you do, that this town is going to make a record this year, but I pray you not to commence in the strain that you apparently have in regard to vacations. I notified Mr. Hermance that all managers, this did not apply to assistant managers, but without a doubt they will also have a vacation, have a vacation of not to exceed ten days the coming summer, leaving on Sunday and returning to be in the store not later than the Saturday morning, giving them a full ten to twelve days. I could not think of allowing you to come East the present summer, but shall be very pleased to after you have put in a full year at the Portland store, and show me just what can be done out there and I want you to feel contented to remain there until then. These trips of a month or more only leave eleven months in the year and we do not feel that we can spare good men this length of time.

Trust that you will realize our wise decision in the matter and that I may hear from you in the same enthusiastic weekly letter that I have been in the habit of getting.

Yours very truly,
[E. P. Charlton]

3.

Fall River, Mass.
March 19, 1909

Mr. Simon Kapstein,
c/o The E. P. Charlton & Co.,
Seattle, Wash.

My dear Kapstein:

When you get to Portland, go at things diplomatically, so not to have any friction with Mr. Baldwin. Would suggest and get the store in perfect shape and the counters and shelvings stained and fixed up, so that they will look smart and snappy.

Also see where the trouble is on this salary end. It is at least $50.00 a week more than it should be for the amount of business. Why Tacoma can do the business they do on one-half the salary expenditure is more than I know. See if you can find out where the leakages are, and suggest some way to get this down or bring the business up to where it should be for this salary expenditure. Not that I am complaining about the Portland business—Mr. Baldwin has shown himself a money-maker and a good manager, but there is always room for improvement and when a store shows that it can do the business this does during the month of December, it certainly can do more every week in the year, that is what I mean.

Keep your eyes open and post me continually on conditions everywhere.

Yours truly,
E. P. CHARLTON
Signature dictated.

4.

Fall River, Mass.
April 2, 1909

Mr. Simon Kapstein,
c/o The E. P. Charlton & Co.,
Bellingham, Wash.

My dear Kapstein:

Yours to hand and noted. This will, no doubt, find you in Bellingham. Am glad you like Mr. Taber. I felt every confidence in him before he left. I feel that he will increase this business, and ultimately bring it on to a sound paying basis.

You are in a city now which is a great disappointment to me. Do you realize that this town is 38,000 to 40,000. Have just got the correct census from Bradstreet, which gives it at 38,000—4,000 larger than New Britain, Ct.: 10,000 larger than New London and Norwich, and here is a man doing $400.00 or less a week. It is management, lack of merchandise and everything else. This store should do not less than $750.00 to $800.00 at the least. Now, what is it? Isherwood is a nice boy but he has been positively "dead" and I am afraid, even though you shake him up and get the store in condition he will allow it to drop off again. Is he there early in the morning and looking out for business? He wrote me a letter in regard to getting into the game and showing me that this store could be the leader in Class 5. It most assuredly should be and is belongs in Class 4 on account of population.

What do you hear of Brittan? How is he doing? Is he going to make good in his post card shop? No doubt, he will be able to make a living during this year, as it is Fair time and there are plenty of souvenirs and other things he can get hold of.

Yours truly,

E. P. CHARLTON
Signature dictated. EPC/MD.

5.

Fall River, Mass.
April 8, 1909

Mr. Simon Kapstein,
c/o The E. P. Charlton & Co.,
Bellingham, Wash.

Dear Simon:

Would like to have you remain in Bellingham until you receive instructions to leave. Think this will be the best way for you to do in every instance. We will then be in a position always to put our hands on you as available at a moments notice.

Would like to have Bellingham gotten in shape and the sales increased to a size commensurate with the population of the town. There is no question about there needing goods-- I have written this repeatedly. Make a showing of specials in the window as soon as you have other goods to sell the people when the specials draw them in.

Bellingham should do $1,000.00 per week and I will not be satisfied until the store gets there.

Yours truly,

E. P. CHARLTON
Signature dictated.
EPC/MD.

[*In MS*: Be careful & place order into Seattle for everything this store needs which S can share.]

6.

Bellingham, Wash.,
4/14/1909

Mr. E. P. Charlton
Fall River, Mass.

My dear Mr. Charlton:

Yours of the 8th, inst. received and noted. Intended to leave this noon but will not until further instruction from you. Store is looking good. This store will not do a $1000.00 a week this year. but venture to state that it will develop to it in a year or so. [*The following crossed out:* Isherwood is getting along nicely. To do $1000.00 a week it must have a larger assortment of goods and that will mean to increase our counter space.] However I'll do the best I can and keep things going. [*The following crossed out*: and look to accomplish that goal.] Isherwood is getting along nicely. Awaiting a reply, I am.

Sincerely yours,
Simon Kapstein

7.

Fall River, Mass.
April 15, 1909

Mr. Simon Kapstein,
c/o The E. P. Charlton & Co.,
Bellingham, Wash.

My dear Kapstein:

We shall make a change in Vancouver, Mr. Upton leaving on the 10th. You will have to be there by the first. Shall make a change as soon as possible with Mr. Isherwood, but cannot just at present. Give the boy a good, strong talking to on ordering out his goods, and putting snap into this business. Good windows and good looking merchandise on his counters.

When you are in Vancouver, you will have to get a careful line on the way Mr. Upton has been running his business, also upon his record while there. If honest inventory was taken, he made a fine showing last year, showing that he knows how to mark goods to get the right percentage in Canada. Remember you are not in the U.S. when you go there, and goods must be marked to show about the same relative per cent that he has been showing, namely 56% to 58%.

He claims his health is failing and cannot stand the climate. There is no finer climate in the word than Vancouver.

I want you to get this store into perfect shape, if it is not, and write me, giving me your opinion of all the weak points. This store should be one of the best paying in Canada, and made a fine showing for the six months last year. You will have to remain until the new manager arrives, provided he does not before Mr. Upton leaves.

My opinion is that it is his wife that is back of all his trouble; that she is urging him to go back into the southern part of California and has been a load ever since he married her. This, of course, is confidential. I shall either put Mr. Spence of Butte or Mr. Arnott of San Bernardino in there.

Yours truly,
E. P. CHARLTON
Dictated Signature.
EPC/MD.

8.

Fall River, Mass.
May 24, 1909

Mr. Simon Kapstein,
c/o The E. P. Charlton & CO., Ltd.,
Vancouver, B. C.

Dear Simon:

In reply to your numerous letters, I should most assuredly get rid of this assistant that you claim is deficient. Do not wait for instructions, but clean out the undesirable help and get in men who have good records, and that you are positive have recommendations that are valid. Mr. Taber has been successful, he tells me, in getting one or two first-class men. The Seattle business shows what good management can do.

Also glad to see Isherwood picking up. I know what these stores should do normally. There is no reason why Bellingham should not do $800.00 a week; Walla Walla, $500.00 and Vancouver, $2,000.00. Do not like to see you drop this store down below $200.00 any day. It must be staples that you need. Keep the orders coming in where necessary and we will have them filled promptly.

I trust to have a manager there within the next four weeks, and after a stay of ten days with him, you will go to Portland for two or three weeks at least. I want to have you size this store up and give your attention to it, as I believe we are doing only one-half the business we can in Portland today, as big as the increase is that they are continually making. We do not half know what we can do in this business, Simon, by careful management and stock keeping.

Yours truly,
E. P. CHARLTON
Dictated Signature.
EPC/MD.

9.

Fall River, Mass.
May 26, 1909

Mr. Simon Kapstein,
c/o E. P. Charlton & Co., Ltd.,
Vancouver, B.C.

My dear Kapstein:

I am in receipt of letter today from Mr. Royal T. Twombly, the young man you doubtless discharged, who was assistant to Mr. Upton, who states that he refused to substantiate a false statement touching upon the character of Mr. Upton, at your request. Now, I wish no controversy between you and him, but want your explanation as to the above.

I also received a letter from Mr. Upton who stated that he had not resigned and wished to continue in the Company, and asked us to reinstate him in a southern store, which I propose to do at the earliest opportunity, if he is satisfied with the proposition we make. He also stated that the reason he left Vancouver in two days was because you showed very clearly that you did not need his services, and he could be of no use to you. Now, Simon, let this be a lesson in the future. You have a certain amount of authority and supervision, but never show it on entering a store with a manager, or in taking the place of one removed. Go about this work diplomatically, making the manager feel that you came to assist him; that you are dependent somewhat upon his advice in regard to local matters; that you want his assistance, and make the manager feel when you are in the capacity of inspector that you came there only to assist him and suggest. Some managers are very set in their ways and they take offense at a man coming in and pulling their stock to pieces and saying, "Here, this is not right, "that is not right". You may not know the conditions of the town. The way to go about it is to state that, Los Angeles or Seattle, or Tacoma have been following out this or that method of showing goods and made a big success of it, and instruct the girls and the managers as to how you would like the work done. In this way, you can get good results all around, whereas on the other hand, the manager will antagonize you and the moment you are out, doubtless, put the goods back as they were before. If you can show him conclusively that it is profitable to do as you suggest, then there will be a benefit all around.

You realize that we want no manufactured evidence against any of our men. We want, and are glad, to know that they are spoken of highly. What we want to know is, if they are or are not a credit to the Company and desirable employees.

You state in your previous letter that Mr. Upton had been on the point of discharging this man a number of times, but never felt that he could get hold of any one as dependable. Now, I shall want this verified, of course. We do not propose to keep undesirable people in our employ a day, neither do we propose to discharge any straight, honest, capable man or woman who has been in our employ. I trust I have made myself plain and that in the future you will be governed by my advice.

Yours sincerely,
[*signed*] E. P. Charlton
MD.

10.

Fall River, Mass.
June 1, 1909

Mr. Simon Kapstein,
c/o E. P. Charlton & Co., Ltd.,
Vancouver, B. C.

My dear Simon:

Mr. Holcombe of San Diego will arrive in Vancouver about the 15th to take charge of the Vancouver store. I want you to put him through every course of training in regard to the entry of goods through Customs, the marking of merchandise, keeping up of stock and the difference between the general customs in Canada and the U.S. Size him up well and stay with him until you think he is competent to manage this store.

Then, I shall want you to put in two or three days in Bellingham again and a week in Walla Walla, also a week in Portland. May possibly find it necessary for you to leave for Salt Lake previous to this, if we can get our store there in shape to open. If there is time, between the Salt Lake opening, or after it, for a two weeks vacation for you, not to exceed this this year, you will be at liberty to take it. I know you have earned it and deserve it, but business is on the jump this year and we do not want to throw away any of the good opportunities to keep it rolling, now that it is once started.

I trust to see the Vancouver store up to $1500.00 or $1600.00 a week before the first of July. Of course, the Seattle Fair will materially benefit Vancouver, as well as the other stores.

Yours very truly,
E. P. CHARLTON.
Signature dictated.
EPC/MD

11.

Fall River, Mass.
May 24, 1910

Mr. Simon Kapstein,
c/o E. P. Charlton & Co.,
San Francisco, Calif.

My dear Simon:

I am in receipt of yours of the 12th and do not believe that it would be any money in our pocket to keep our music or candy department open provided the Pacific Syndicate and other stores in our line closed. This is foolishness in any instance. I will fight hard against the Saturday closing act in any city, as I think it is suicidal for our business, but when it comes to a matter of keeping open every evening, I think it is foolishness, unless your competitors do.

I trust to have things straightened out so that I can get you on the move very soon. With the new store at Aberdeen and Salem coming on, I want you in the North just as soon as I can get you there. Will advise you, however, if possible, in advance, of any change we make.

Yours truly,
E. P. CHARLTON.
Dictated Signature.
EPC/MD.

12.

Fall River, Mass.
May 26, 1910

Mr. Simon Kapstein,
c/o E. P. Charlton & Co.,
San Francisco, Calif.

My dear Simon:

I am in receipt of yours of the 19th, and realize that what you say is absolutely correct about the Market St. store,. If it is possible for you to put a little work in for us there at odd times, I wish you would do so. I have written a letter to Mr. Hermance today and told him that I should have to insist that he give up all outside work for the next few months, until we could get this store into shape. There is no reason that a bank deficit of $23,000.00 should not have goods to make life; specials in the windows at all times with the right price on them; snappily arranged in the way they should be, there is nothing like staples continually shown. This leader business is all foolishness, if you have not got the merchandise back of you to attractively show and to interest the people. It is staple goods that people want, at the right price, and I believe there is plenty of merchandise in that store at from $10.00 to $12.50, which, if sold at 10¢, would create interest.

What we want is to get some of the money out of this overstock of merchandise, and we shall be most pleased to put leaders in. The trouble is that there are goods on the counters improperly and poorly shown, with a line of merchandise in the basement that would fill up a ten acre space attractively. I am disgusted with the way [*crossed out*: this matter; *in MS*: and manner this store*] is being run, and if you can do anything to assist Mr. Hermance in getting this store where it belongs, I shall most certainly appreciate it.

Your statement of "lack of life" exactly expresses it. It is what the store has always lacked and it is a perfect shame that a store opening with the bright prospects that this did has run down in the manner it has. It has, of course, been absolutely impossible for Mr. Hermance to give it only a limited amount of attention, and I trust that when he starts in and makes it a life business for the next few months, that we can get hold of the reins again.

Yours truly,
E. P. CHARLTON.
Signature dictated.
EPC/MD.

13.

Fall River, Mass.
July 19, 1910

Mr. Simon Kapstein,
c/o E. P. Charlton & Co.,
San Francisco, Calif.

My dear Simon:

I am in receipt of letter from you regarding settlement made by our Miss Morrison. It is just as broad as it is long, my boy, and the settlement on January first will be made in accordance with percentage basis. Last year on account of profits made from stores you visited, your percentage was far above what we expected. We hope it will be more this year, though you will now be based entirely upon a per cent of the entire company. If you are located permanently after the first of the year, probably different arrangements will be made. If you need this $137.00, we shall be pleased to send it to you, and think that I will give instructions now for Miss Morrison to do so, but you can readily understand that we have to base your salary on the amount of money paid you. It does not make any difference whether it is for expenses, allowance of so much per day, or what, your services will be figured on a certain per cent of the profits, and it depends on you how economical you are, or how extravagant.

Yours very truly,
E. P. CHARLTON.
Signature dictated.
EPC/MD.

14.

Fall River, Mass.
July 30, 1910

Mr. Simon Kapstein,
c/o E. P. Charlton & Co.,
San Francisco, Calif.

My dear Simon:

I am pleased to note the steady improvement in Market St. If you can get this business up to the $3,000.00 mark, you will have accomplished big results and put this store on a self-sustaining and paying basis. The first thing to do is to eliminate the $15,000 to $18,000 of bank deficit by big sales and pushes on apparent overstocks, or dead stocks. If there are, get them out and get them into money. I want to see this store, by the first of December, with not to exceed a $10,000.00 deficit. Try your best to accomplish something each week on this.

Yours truly,
E. P. CHARLTON.
Signature dictated.
EPC/MD.

15.

Fall River, Mass.
October 3, 1910

Mr. Simon Kapstein,
c/o E. P. Charlton & Co.,
Portland, Oregon.

Dear Simon:

I am in receipt of yours of the 28th, and very glad that you have hold of this store and can work out some new and original ideas. I was at a loss to know just what condition the store was in as far as the new part was concerned and how much of a handicap this was. As I understand, it is going to make a nice, clean department, as per our plans and drawings sent out. Look them over and see if they have been followed out.

When there is a free circulation of trade from one to the other, and jewelry, candy, etc. shown up in the proper manner, there is no reason why this store should not take No. 1 place. Mr. Obertin has been waiting for this for some time. Another thing, I want you to weed out the unnecessary men in the basement and cut this salary account down to where it should be. If they can do $1,000.00 to $1500.00 more per week, as they should, the salary account is all right, otherwise, abnormally high.

Should put in a lot of new ideas for showing merchandise. The 8 inch plate glass dividers, cross section, with two small pieces, piling up a gross of tooth-brushes, combs, hair brushes, toilet goods, etc.; by properly tagging these, we have found, this adds immensely to the sale of these goods. For instance, we had rubber heels, wired together. We dumped them in one of these compartments, and showed rubber heels beside them in boxes, selling ten to one shown up in bulk to those, each pair in a box.

I think it would be a good plan to get all hands around for one evening and a full day, even a day longer than this, if necessary, after the connection is completed. Have fixtures put in, rearrange the store for new, fresh windows of big values and big signs, "Opening of the new store, and see if you cannot start things in with a rush. $1,000.00 a day should be a normal business for this store, and unless Mr. Baldwin can get it up there, it will not pay for the added expense you are under.

I want you to show me the benefit of your time and ability there in the same manner that you did previously. It has been my opinion that you gave this store a good start before. I can prove this conclusively, if it forges ahead now that you are putting in another session with Mr. Baldwin.

I am very sorry that Mr. Barstow had to be dispensed with. I think he would have made a valuable man under Mr. Baldwin, much better than his son Pere, whose habits I wish you to look into carefully, as well as his brother's, and write me confidentially your opinion as to their worth. My idea is that it would be much better for Mr. Baldwin to have less of his family in the store.

Write me every few days in regard to the way things are going along, and if possible, want you to remain there until after their big opening.

We have sent Mr. Sproule from Fall River to store 42. He will arrive there in about ten days.

Yours truly,
[*initialed*: EPC] E. P. CHARLTON.
Signature dictated.
EPC/MD.

16.

Fall River, Mass.
October 10, 1910

Mr. Simon Kapstein,
c/o E. P. Charlton & Co.,
Portland, Oregon.

My dear Simon:

I am in receipt of your communication relative to condition of store, etc., and thoroughly agree with you as to the advisability of so many of the family working for their own father. It is absolutely not to his interest nor to ours, and if you can diplomatically make him understand that this must be changed, it will perhaps save a great deal of friction and hard feelings. I am perfectly willing that the young man who was there when I visited the store, be it Myron or the other one, may remain, but I will have only one of these boys in the Portland store. When their father has so little influence over them, and a moral man such as he is, and the boys will come in there and smoke in the store, it shows conclusively that they are not wanted by me at least, and I exceedingly regret that he took it upon himself to do this without sanction from this office. Mr. Barstow would have been worth more to him as far as work goes than both of these boys, in my opinion. If Mr. Barstow had wanted to stay with us, he could have had Aberdeen, but not at any $30.00 a week. We are hiring men on their own merits and divide profits with them and he can never draw out of any store we have to exceed $20.00, and he has got to show us that he can make good. Possibly I may try to do something for him later on, if he keeps straight and is inclined to go back into the business.

I have now another pleasant little mess to clean up in Salem. I sent Miss Lottie Kimball out there (you remember her) more for her health than anything else. She has discovered a state of affairs which I thought existed but was not sure. If you find that this Mr. Ohiser has drawn out, in addition to $28.00, another $10.00 in cash, from the till, I want him relieved from management and take his keys, unless after talking with Miss Kimball, you decide this is inexpedient. We will send out another man to take his place as soon as possible, unless you can give them a good, bright boy from Portland at $10.00 or $12.00 a week to go out there and help Miss Kimball, one who can dress windows, open freight and check it. I much prefer having her there than the present manager. He is a single man who cannot get along with $20.00 a week and has to borrow money out of the till. We certainly can get along with [*in MS*: out] him.

Try to put in a couple of days at Salem and help Miss Kimball straighten out the store in good shape. I enclose you letter to give to Mr. Ohiser, if you decide on making this change.

In his letter to me, he stated that he drew $28.00 to pay his doctor's bills. It would be a good plan to see the receipted bills for this $28.00. Another item he has entered on report is $30.00 for advertising. Look into this also. We never allow for advertising, and he has again taken a responsibility to use our funds.

Yours very truly,
[*signed*]   E. P. CHARLTON.
MD.

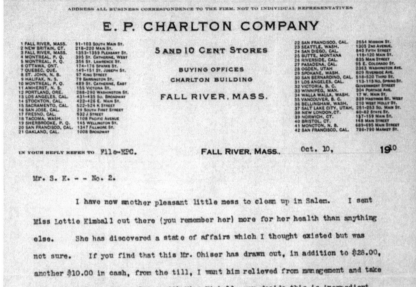

Fig. 24. Document 16, page 2, October 10, 1910. Note that the letterhead lists forty-two stores.

17.

Fall River, Mass.
October 13, 1910

Mr. Simon Kapstein,
c/o E. P. Charlton & Co.,
Portland, Oregon.

Dear Simon:

I am in receipt of yours of the 7th. I wrote you in reference to these matters last week. I want you to give me candid, impartial reports on everything just as you see them there. I am not at all satisfied with Portland. Although I have striven for months to feel that we were doing the best we could with this city, I do not believe it, and I am less satisfied since Mr. Baldwin has seen fit to take two of his sons in there and discharge a good worker such as Mr. Barstow, who he was instrumental in taking on against my instructions in the first place, but as far as work is concerned, and if he has a good man over him, Barstow is worth half a dozen ordinary men as a stock keeper. I am not satisfied to have the boys have the run of the office, and I am less satisfied with the expense account they are now under. It should be cut 25% to 30% and at the same time, do more business. Unless it is essential, I want you to remain there until the thing is lined up so that you feel certain it is going all right.

This Stevenson, whom I met and liked very much, is a good, bright, young man and will, no doubt, drop into a management, but don't you think it poor policy on your part to think of taking him out as a manager? Who has Mr. Baldwin then that he can depend upon with any executive ability? If I am not right, I want you to post me. I wanted you to stay there until you had this annex all finished with fixtures in and a good opening, and see if we cannot get the business up to where it belongs, namely $1,000.00 a day, which this store should do, any and every day in the week; from $1500.00 to $2000.00 on Saturday.

Ed has been here with his pretty, new wife. She, apparently, is all the boy could desire in the way of a help-mate, and I trust he will be very happy and prosperous.

Yours truly,
E. P. CHARLTON.
Signature dictated.
EPC/MD.

18.

Fall River, Mass.
October 24, 1910

Mr. Simon Kapstein,
c/o E. P. Charlton & Co.,
Portland, Oregon.

My dear Simon:

I am in receipt of yours of the 18th regarding Salem and Portland stores. I think one of your shortcomings is lack of what the poor surgeon has - the nerve and confidence to cut deep.

I trust that you are right about this Ohiser, but I put very little stock in it, and my opinion is that the best thing for him and ourselves would have been to have let him go. In the first place, you should have found out what became of this $38.00 besides $20.00 a week that he has been drawing. Any boy that would forget himself after being put in the management of a store, the first few months, and spend the best part of his time away from business, will not improve. He may be more careful about being discovered, but he will still be dishonest. [*In MS*: If he has left the store to run itself,] He is a thief, pure and simple, for he is taking the time which belongs to the Company and might have caused, and may have caused us big losses by so doing. First impression is everything, and this store has been left in a run-down condition.

If nothing else is done until the first of the year, I should give Miss Kimball entire charge of the cash. He is to draw not to exceed $15.00 a week from now until January first; have this thoroughly understood; $12.00 would be better.

I believe it is a good little town and can be made a money-maker, if properly managed. I am looking forward to the boom of opening Portland, with the expectation of seeing that come somewhere within reach of figures it should do every week. There are a number of stores in the different syndicates which are not as well located and have not the people that Portland has as shoppers, who are doing $35,000.00 to $50,000.00 per month.

Yours truly,
E. P. CHARLTON.
Signature dictated.
EPC/MD.

19.

Fall River, Mass.
November 2, 1910

Mr. Simon Kapstein,
c/o E. P. Charlton & Co.,
Portland, Oregon.

Dear Simon:

We are sending Mr. Baldwin's letter to you, so that if you deem it advisable, and Mr. Baldwin has not returned, you can take the matter up with Messrs. Veasie & Veasie, Corbett Building, who, Mr. Baldwin states, are our attorneys there. See that our contract is lived up to, to the letter, and checks presented for rent to Mr Yeon, when due, before witnesses.

Yours truly,
E. P. CHARLTON.
Dictated Signature.
EPC/MD.

20.

Fall River, Mass.
Nov. 23, 1910

Mr. Simon Kapstein,
c/o E. P. Charlton & Co.,
Portland, Oregon.

My dear Simon:

I am in receipt of yours of the 13th, and regret that it will be impossible for you to go South to take your Masonic Degree before the first of the year. Do not see how you are going to get away, as either Mr. Bardel or myself will be out there the latter part of December. There will be the Everett inventory to take, change of management, also a block to build in Bellingham, and I want you to keep watch of things carefully in Portland through December. Think you can add a good slice to your salary by helping out in this store, where you will be ready to be called upon at a moment's notice, if anything goes wrong in the northwest.

Trust this will be perfectly agreeable to youself.

With best wishes, I am,

Yours truly,
E. P. CHARLTON.
Dictated Signature.
EPC/MD.

21.

Fall River, Mass.
Jan. 28, 1911

Mr. Simon Kapstein,
c/o E. P. Charlton & Co.,
Everett, Wash.

My dear Simon:

Enclosed check balances your account for the year 1910, as per vote by the Board of Directors, Jan. 1st. I trust, my boy, that you are putting your money in safe investments and not in any "wild-cat" schemes.

I can give you no encouragement the present year of being able to place you in a permanent location. I do not see the opening for you to make any such amount of money or to be of any such assistance to us as you are in the capacity of inspector. I trust that Mr. Bardol has talked this matter over with you. I want you to realize that we appreciate your services and have the greatest interest in your future and your welfare. In an organization of this kind, there must be experts in every department. These changes will come in good time and I want you to allow me to be the judge of where and when to place you.

Let me hear from you in a good, long letter on the Everett store and the capabilities of Mr. Busher and what you think the prospects are. We have yet to receive the first days sales and I am awaiting them with considerable anxiety. One thing that should be made clear to Mr. Busher is that we shall expect the sales in this store to equal and exceed those of Landers, which should be easy.

Yours very truly,
[*signed*] E. P. CHARLTON.
MD/

22.

Fall River, Mass.
April 6, 1911

Mr. Simon Kapstein,
c/o E. P. Charlton & Co.,
Walla Walla, Wash.

Dear Sir:

We wrote you sometime ago to go to Walla Walla from Boise, and from there to Spokane, from Spokane to Butte, stopping at Missoula. Recently there has developed some sort of friction between the manager and his assistant at Butte, and there evidently is some trouble, which we want you to look into, and on this account, we want you to go direct from Walla Walla to Butte, without stopping at Spokane, so the manager at Spokane will not know that you are going to Butte, and drop in on them and stay there until we write you further, and get this store into shape.

Look into everything very carefully. Have a talk with the assistant confidentially, as well as with the manager on the other hand, confidentially, and make inquiries around, giving us a detailed report of the situation as you find it.

You might also look the stock over and see if you find any merchandise there that is not listed, goods that may have been bought locally. See what has been bought from the Butte Paper Co., and report. Incidentally, without exciting any suspicion, ask about the perfumes that are in baskets in the basement. See where they came from, who they were bought from and if there is a charge on the books of their having been paid for, and report in detail on this transaction.

This is an opportunity for you to display your tact and diplomacy in handling this matter. We know nothing detrimental to either of these men absolutely, but we shall depend upon you to look into the situation very carefully, and after you have spent a sufficient amount of time on it, so that you know exactly what you are talking about, we shall expect to hear from you.

You will write us immediately on leaving Walla Walla, so that we may know where to reach you by wire.

Yours very truly,
E. P. CHARLTON COMPANY
BY [*signed*] E. A. Bardol
V.P.

MD

23.

Fall River, Mass.
April 7, 1911

Mr. Simon Kapstein,
c/o E. P. Charlton Company,
Butte, Montana.

Dear Sir:

We wrote you yesterday at Walla Walla, with reference to the Butte store, and copy of the letter is herewith enclosed. We were prompted in doing this by <u>confidential</u> letters, which we received from Mr. Williams, the assistant manager, indicating that everything at Butte was not exactly correct and in accordance with our wishes.

We were informed by telegraph this morning from the First National Bank, that our manager is not giving proper attention to the business and is absent from the store several days, etc., and Mr. Williams wires that Sprungman is drinking heavily and has left town to sober up, that he is guarding our interests. We have wired to Mr. Sprungman, suspending him for the present and to have him turn over all papers and keys to Mr. Williams. We have wired Mr. Williams to take temporary charge of the store and of our interests, until further advised. We have also written to the Bank, thanking them for their interest in advising us.

The telegram sent you to Walla Walla was urgent to have you immediately leave for Butte. We want you now to take charge of the Butte store until further notice. Look into every detail and report to Mr. Charlton carefully exactly what you find has been the condition in the past and suggest any remedy and improvements that will be of advantage to the business, as soon as you have concluded in your mind what that should be.

Mr. Williams intimates to us that the business done at Butte is not what it should be, that there is a possibility of doing a much larger business but that Mr. Sprungman has neglected it to a large extent. You may also find that the help proposition wants weeding out and cleaning up and that we want courteous, lady-like people and nothing else. This store above all that we have should command the very highest class of lady clerks. They should be capable, they should be clean-cut, be well recommended and thoroughly experienced, because we pay them the Union scale of wages, which is as much as they can get anywhere, and we are in position to be the dictators far more so than we could expect to be in any other store that we operate, and on this account, I would suggest that you spare no time in selecting a class of help that will be a credit to the establishment, and that they be drilled to know that we are in Butte to do business with everybody and that everybody is entitled to the same courteous treatment, whether they are buyers or only shoppers.

Look into the office situation. See if there has been any irregularity. Make careful comparison of the deposits and the sales with the registers and see if everything has been regular. The young lady in the office, I found, is one that has been with us since we opened the store and appeared to be very ladylike. Further than this, I know nothing about her.

The store may require some rearrangement and improvement, but the most vital thing at this time before you are the facts above outlined. We will consider the painting and fixings after this has all been cleared up.

We very anxiously await some advice from you after you have looked the situation over.

Yours very truly,
E. P. CHARLTON COMPANY
BY [*signed*] E. A. Bardol
                    V.P.
MD

24.

Walla Walla, Wash.
April 7, 1911

Mr. E. P. Charlton
Fall River, Mass.

My dear Mr. Charlton:

Telegram dated April 7, instructing me to take next train to Butte received, and will lea[*in MS*: v]e to-night at 8:15 which will bring me in Saturday, April 8 at 10 P.M. I have Walla Walla Store in pretty good shape, but have done nothing about the basement, which needs thorough overhauling. Have left instruction with Mr. McMurray how to go about his work, and he assured me that instructions would be carried out. He strikes me as being a very nice boy and can almost vouch for his honesty.

Regarding new location, I would say it would not be to our advantage to move out of the block that we are in and would suggest trying to close the Levy's Book Store deal, which no doubt is the best location that can be had in Walla Walla for our business, otherwise we better remain where we are. I have instructed McMurray as soon as he receives any definite answer from Levy, to advise you.

I trust I will find everything in Butte satisfactory and will write you immediately upon arriving there.

Sincerely yours,
[Simon Kapstein]

25.

Butte, Montana
April 13, 1911.

Mr. E. P. Charlton
Fall River, Mass.

My Dear Mr. Charlton:--

Letters under date of April 6th and 7th filed E.A.[*in MS*: B]. received.

I trust you will agree with me that in letting Mr. Sprungman go, as I did was to the best interest of the Company, and protects us from some cheap [*in MS*: "]John lawyer.[*in MS*: "] We have here a force of help to be proud of, all are ladylike, courteous and clean-cut. It would not be to our advantage to make any changes in the help. After thinking over, I thought it would not be doing the young lady justice who refused to tie up with Mr. Sprungman; I further give her credit for doing so. She is a clean-cut girl, honest and of a nice family, and Mr. Sprungman was trying to take advantage of her. After going into several confidential chats with the clerks of the store, I find that Mr. Sprungman has tried to propose to several of the young ladies. If Mr. Sprungman was that weak to allow drink to upset him over a girl, I am sure you or anyone else has no further use for him. Outside of business Sprungman was not living a clean life. He kept a flat of three rooms, which he paid $20.00 a month for, had his own furniture which he bought on the installment plan, for which he paid $20.00 a month, and the dishes which he had at this flat were all from our stock which he claims were paid for, but neither the young lady in the office or Mr. Williams know of this. I advised him to clear out of town at once and he left Tuesday night.

Under separate cover I am mailing you a complete register reading from January 1st, up to date for your benefit. No record was ever kept of the money taken out of the registers, but if registers were short to any great amount, notations were made. I, myself, think that the young lady in the office is a clean-cut little girl and honest. Would not consider any vital improvements, as I think we can get along this year with out it. We are out of a great many good staple articles which I will make up small conservative orders and mail them into the main office. There is no question but that we can do more business here, in fact, we will have to. Will try to reduce the stock which is from $5000.00 to $6000.00 more than it should be. I know that after I have been here four or five weeks, Mr. Williams will be in a position to run the store to our satisfaction, which has not been done in the past. I have no doubt that Sprungman was going from bad to worse and has reached the stage were it would be committing suicide to our business had he remained much longer.

In regards to goods purchased locally from the Butte Paper Co., we have bought from them since January 1st, about $75.00 worth of merchandise, including envelopes, clothespins, copper tacks, clothes lines, dime banks, marbles, ink, shaving brushes, toilet paper, playing cards, etc., all which we paid from 15% to 25% more than we could land them for, and inferior grades at that. These bills were paid for locally and mailed to main office. Mr. Williams, I feel almost certain has told the truth in all that has transpired, taking no chances on the results. The boy is one that we can trust and depend upon. His uncle, who is well known here and who is as fine a gentleman as one cares to meet, told me that while he is absolutely certain of the boy's honesty and sincerety in his work, he will make it a point to see that the boy will continue to live as a man should. Mr. Williams has a very nice little wife and they live in two furnished rooms. He likes the business and takes to it like a fish to water. I can speak only in the highest light of him. All whom I have spoken to and inquired of his recommendation, speak very highly of him.

I am now going about making changes in the store as I see fit and have had all the windows retrimmed since I have arrived.

Upon remaining here a little longer, will write you more. Hoping this will give you a brief outline of local conditions, I beg to remain,

Sincerely yours,
[Simon Kapstein]

26.

Fall River, Mass.
April 18, 1911.

Mr. Simon Kapstein,
c/o E. P. Charlton Company,
Butte, Montana.

Dear Simon:

Yours of the 13th to hand and noted. Am very glad that you have taken hold of the Butte matter as you have, and doubtless, young Williams will make a manager, if he is thoroughly posted and watched over for the next few weeks. There is a big chance for him to show what he is worth. This store has been handicapped by poor management from the start, and I have no doubt whatever that it can be made a paying proposition, by giving it the careful attention that is necessary.

Yours very truly,
[*signed*] E. P. CHARLTON.
Signature dictated.
EPC/MD.

27.

Fall River, Mass.
May 4, 1911.

Mr. Simon Kapstein,
c/o E. P. Charlton Company,
Butte, Montana.

Dear Simon:

I have not written you very often for the past few weeks, as I thought you were busy getting the Butte store into shape. Now, that you are thoroughly confident that this young man can take care of the store in every respect, marking the goods right, and has snap enough to keep things going, I want you to leave immediately for Spokane.

By vote of the Directors this year, it is entirely up to you to materially benefit yourself on present business done on the Pacific Coast this year. I want you to understand that every dollar you make puts so much in your own pocket.

There are two stores that are troubling me considerably, and I want you to get away immediately, or a soon as possible, and go to Spokane and take an inventory of this store. It will not be necessary to disturb sales, as you can simply deduct a fair amount for each day that you are taking the stock [*in MS*: for goods sold after inventory]. In the next place, with basement help, this stock can be arranged and "culls" thrown out, and either put on sale at a price or put into the garbage. We will then be satisfied that the stock that this gentlemen sent in January first was somewhere near accurate. I want two two weeks put in here, and then, on to Portland.

This store with an annex, costing double what it did last year for rent and expenses, is running behind last year in sales. Now, it is either robbery on the part of the employees of cash or merchandise, or Mr. Baldwin is letting things get right away from him. Here is a store that should do not less than $5,000.00 a week, one of the best stands and one of the best cities that we have got in the United States. I want you to go into this matter carefully day after day and solve this problem and let me know where it is. Don't guess at things, but get at the bottom of them. We must get Portland back into the $5,000.00 a week column or else we will be a loser this year. Now, that we have got a new store in San Francisco and with possibilities of getting rid of the old one, it looks as though there would be no loss there during 1911.

I anticipate great results from your visits to these two points. Forward your [*in MS*: Spokane] books on here without extending or adding, and I would suggest taking the stock upstairs [*in MS*: and turning the books] at night and starting in that way, and then taking the basement. In this way, it will not interfere with trade to any great extent. We do not expect accuracy, but want it within $200.00 or $300.00, which may vary on account of taking the counters, etc. in the store, which I do not want you to disturb to any great extent, but be careless in nothing else, however, as we want as nearly an accurate inventory as possible. By doing this in a half way manner, you may work an injury to others.

Yours truly,
[*signed*] E. P. CHARLTON.
MD.

[*In MS*: Be sure that you know <u>quantities</u> and prices are correct in taking this inventory.]

28.

Fall River, Mass.
May 15, 1911.

Mr. Simon Kapstein,
c/o E. P. Charlton & Co.,
Spokane, Wash.,

Dear Simon:

We are in receipt of your wire this morning. It is not necessary to wire us in regard to matters of this kind, although you probably thought it for the best. It costs a dollar and what interest have we on an investment of this kind.

Now, there are a few things that I want to bring clearly to your attention, Simon. We have received a long letter from the cashier of the Butte store, who has made statements that this Williams, who is now manager, is a liar and many other things; that he has taken letters addressed to you out of the waste basket and pieced them together to see their purport, and that she has shown the wife nothing about the cashier end of the business and that she knows nothing. Now I imagine that a great deal of this is talk, and it may be a good plan that she has been eliminated, but I have never thoroughly made up my mind that a man is perfectly conscientious and honest, who undermines another for the sake of securing the position and this is apparently what Williams did in both telegrams and letters. It looks to me as though he was a very sly boy. He may be all right and I hope he is, but your trouble, in my opinion, is that you take too much stock in what these men tell you, that they pat you on the back and make you believe anything.

Now, if you are going to make a success and there are going to be big chances within the next few years, you have got to work for just one concern, and that is, The E. P. Charlton & Co. and the people in this office.

You are now taking the stock of a store, which I trust you will find all right, but a great many things have transpired in Spokane, which have not pleased the writer--an episode in regard to the cashier and one or two other things that were looked up by detectives, at a cost of $100.00 or more, and although, at the time, we had no good reasons to condemn Mr. Files, this stock has never been taken by any one else and we thought it a very good scheme to have this done. We shall continue it in a great many towns, when they least expect it, and in this way, keep close tabs on our real assets. I want these figures put down by you, and I want you to know that the stock is practically there and in a good condition,: that it is packed away and put together in a condition where it can be found;

that goods which are not on sale are put on the counters and that there is a push and a snap given to this business which has heretofore been unknown.

Spokane, as well as Tacoma, and lots of these towns are doing about one-half the business that they should. When I say this, I know that I am right, as towns of the same order [*in MS*: in] Illinois, Dakota, and others, wide ranges apart, with conditions not as good, are doing far more business.

I want you to try to stir these men up, that this is going to be the one of all years when they should make a big showing, carefully figuring on purchasing just the goods that they need, nothing more, and getting their sales up and keeping their expenses down to a minimum.

Be very careful that you get all the bills for merchandise written in on your inventory book, of goods that are taken in stock or have every bill sent on which is included in inventory and clearly marked, so that there may be no mistake in this office on merchandise for which invoices are held up in the Spokane office.

If there are any other good locations up the street or a better location on which you can get an option for a year from now, it would be a good plan to let us know about them, as our lease is expiring at that time and we are trying to get a reasonable figure out of the owners for another term of five or ten years.

Yours very truly,
[*signed*] E. P. CHARLTON.
MD.

29.

Fall River, Mass.
June 14, 1911.

Mr. Simon Kapstein,
c/o E. P. Charlton & Co.,
Spokane, Wash.,

My dear Kapstein:

Books have been received and we are busy now auditing same. Trust that the stock will show up satisfactorily. I want you to keep at this store, my boy, and at this man, not in a superficial way, but get his stock and counters into a solid condition and teach the girls how to keep them up; also a stock man that can keep posted on what is in the basement and not order goods which he already has in stock. Impress upon Mr. Files the necessity of getting his bank balance out of the hole at once and to order conservatively and in smaller quantities from now on, but to keep up the staple line of notions and hardware at all times. His capital is more than sufficient to give him a stock of merchandise, including every saleable item we handle. This store should do a business of 25% to 50% more than it is doing.

For your own interest, I wish that you might cut out vacations this summer. I cannot go into details, but it will make a remarkable difference in your future what these stores net this year. Everything will be changed on the first of the year and strict percentages on given territory on sales only will be followed out with regular contracts.

I have relieved Mr. Baldwin from Boise. Mr. Crowther is now there, and I think, Macomber. This man, I found, was coming in at 10 and 11 o'clock in the morning and had gone twice to Portland, spending three or four days, without notifying this office. The store is not doing one-half the business it should. The idea of a town like Boise doing less than the little town of Moncton and Amherst. It is ridiculous. It should do $1000.00 to $1100.00 a week very easily.

Now, the job in front of you is a big one and the most essential of anything in the line of work we have ever offered you. It would appear to me that "like father, like son" is the case with young Baldwin. Either they are stealing wholesale or the business is getting away from L. M. Baldwin [*in MS*: of Portland]. The idea of a magnificent store located as Portland is, with three times the floor room on the first floor, doing less business they they were last year. There is something very, very wrong, and I believe it is wholly with the management. this store should do on an average of $800.00 to $1,000.00, and on Saturdays, $1200.00 to $1500.00 easily. Now it is up to you to make the showing of your life, by going in as assistant manager and I shall dictate a policy to Mr. Baldwin, whereby your recommendations will be carried out until proved ineffective.

I do not believe the man is paying attention to business. I do not think the windows are snappy. I should cover them with strip posters. Put attractive specials in the window and watch the floor like a cat does a mouse and the sales slips for each register. The first thing, when you go in there, get up a schedule book yourself privately and take down every register. Read these carefully yourself on Sunday and see how they compare. Have slips for every clerk and relieve those who are not doing business. Get a basis and then start clerks in, the regulars, on a bonus of 2% [*in MS*: on] additional [*crossed out*: on their sales; *in MS*: sales over amount they have averaged for three weeks,] after cleaning out all unnecessary help, getting the salaries down to a basis of not more than 7%. This is your first work. The help figures would be all right, if they were doing a business of $6,000.00 a week.

If you will bring this store out with a larger profit even than last year, when we had all the expense of opening, as well as the new store, on our hands for seven months, I will see that you are rewarded by an additional $1,000.00. This is to be entirely confidential. This store should net $75,000.00 to $80,000.00, and it is disgusting to see the business they are doing.

After you have thoroughly studied the situation, give me your ideas. I believe that with proper management that in four weeks time, the business can be doubled.

Now, my plan for you is, if you are all tired out, go into the Yellowstone to some nice little hotel and spend a week after leaving Spokane. As far as chasing around the country for a vacation is concerned, there is no rest in it and it will do you no good. This will put you in good shape to tackle the Portland job.

Do not leave Spokane until you have gotten it where it belongs and until you hear from us on the report.

On the merchandise bills coming in yesterday, there was no data. These should all have been marked "included in inventory". In this way we would have known just how to have figured these merchandise bills [*in MS*: in the Invt.] Trust you did not forget this. If you did, it is a big error, as there is no total of invoices in the books of bills which have been checked and included in inventory, with the exception of a few Borgfeldt's which have been paid.

Yours very truly,
[*signed*] E. P. CHARLTON.
MD.

30.

Fall River, Mass.
July 10, 1911.

Mr. Simon Kapstein,
c/o E. P. Charlton & Co.,
Spokane, Wash.,

Dear Simon:

Just as soon as you take this little vacation we were talking about, if you feel that you need it, I want you to report to Mr. Baldwin and show him the enclosed note. I want you to use every bit of your diplomacy and eye-sight in trying to figure out why our store is not doing double the business.

Do all you can to assist Mr. Baldwin in getting this back into shape. We have notified him, under no circumstances, to hire the Boise manager in this store, nor will we have it. Also, want to know what Mr. Baldwin's habits are in regard to getting to the store mornings, and whether he is kept at his office or among his trade. This in itself would be enough to ruin the business in time.

I want careful attention given to every detail, and reports made to me as often as possible. This is too expensive and profitable a store to have lose ground, and there is no condition in the Northwest which would warrant the Portland store, with their extra space, not doing an increased business.

Taber claims that this back store is worse than the second floor. Although the entrance may be small, this is nonsense. People will walk through an opening into another large room quicker than they will go up stairs, and if the proper musical program and singing is given them, and attractions, they will soon fill the 5th Ave. store with people.

Just mention to Files now to kindly see that this store from now on is kept in this manner. His sales must be kept up, also his stock, and say to him that he must be on the floor every minute possible, and it will be simply up to him whether he is to continue with E. P. Charlton Company after the first of the year or not.

If business does not build up from now on there will be a change before the first of the year.

With best wishes, I am,

Yours very truly,
E. P. CHARLTON.
Dict.Sig.
Steno.2.

31.

Spokane, Wash.,
July 17, 1911

Mr. E. P. Charlton
Fall River, Mass.

My Dear Mr. Charlton:-

Your letter of July 10th received. Will plan to leave Spokane on July 19th and report to Mr. Baldwin on July 24th, this will give me three days vacation. We have received several cases of notions and small wares and thought it best to remain a few days longer to see that it was gotten out and put on sale. Am also having a notion window trimmed and will see that all windows are changed before I leave. I had a chat with Mr. Files on the subject mentioned in your several letters and he promised to give the store better attention. We are expecting a car of tin and enamel ware any day and with this line of merchandise there is no reason why our business should not loom up as we have been out of enamel ware for sometime. My one regret is that I could not put the store on better fottings [*i.e.,* footings] before I left although I worked hard to do it but I however, leave with the satisfaction of knowing that the store and stock room are a hundred percent in better shape than when I took hold and there is no reason Mr. Files should not keep it in such conditions at all times. Have instructed Mr. Files to absolutely cut out buying and order just what he absolutely needs to fill in from time to time. Mr. Files has recently bought a piece of real estate paying $5,000.00 at the following terms: $500 cash; $2,500 March 1st, 1912, and $2,000 March lst, 1913. He tried to interest me in a timber claim of his whereby he asked the loan of $300. and after I refused him this amount he loaned it from a travelling salesman. I can assure you of doing my utmost to carry out your plans at our Portland branch and will report to you at least once a week if not oftener.

With best wishes, I remain,
Sincerely yours,
[Simon Kapstein]

32.

Fall River, Mass.
August 14, 1911.

Mr. Simon Kapstein,
c/o E. P. Charlton Company,
Portland, Oregon.

My dear Simon:

I am in receipt of your numerous letters and glad that you looked over Victoria, Seattle and Vancouver. Your are perfectly correct in your statement that the Northwest is the coming country and we shall locate just as fast as we can get desirable locations.

I wish you had sized up Victoria a little better. That town is worthy of a first-class store with two entrances and it seems as though the proper time to locate it is now, while things are a little bit contracted and dull.

I do not think it is necessary for me to tell you, Simon, that to a considerable extent your future will be effected by the success you have now in Portland--not that you have not been a valuable asset and there will always be a good position for you as long as this firm exists or its successors, if there ever are any, but it will show me clearly that it is your ability alone, if this store now doubles its business and gets into the position where it belongs. If you remember, it ran down in bad shape some years ago, and I put you there for six months and the store commenced to flourish. I gave you a great deal of the credit but conditions may have been the essential cause of the increase in sales. However, I have decided to put you back there now and watch results, for I believe that there is no city on the Coast the equal of Portland, and if New Orleans can do $400,000.00 worth of business in a store half the size of Portland, I see no reason why this store should not do $300,000.00 easily, in fact I believe it is a better, all-around business city than New Orleans is. There is no comparison from bank clearings, as New Orleans is a tremendous seaport while Portland is not.

Your candies in Portland should be bought and sold to net not less than 65% to 70%. If you have got $1200.00 worth of old candies, either have them made over immediately or put them on sale, what will sell, at 5¢ a pound, but get this into money and buy only from week to week, good, fresh goods.

Get the music business where it belongs. Here was a store doing a music business of $300.00 or $400.00 a week, and now shows a gross profit of $292.00. This is nothing. Where has the business gone to? My opinion is that his wife's notoriety in connection with the girls who are singing in the local theatres is the reason for a great many of the popular pieces being thrown out and that this is the prime cause of the dropping off in this department. There has been too much "Salvation Army" in the proceedings all the way through and too little business. The stock of music now is $400.00 more than it should be, and I want you to make an extra effort to use this as a drawing card in getting the people into the Fourth St. store. Also let me know by actual count of cashier, the number of customers you have in the store at say three o'clock each afternoon, both in the Main store and the Fourth St. store. The claim has been that you cannot get the people through, but when they are doing less business with these two magnificent stores on the ground floor, there is some reason for it. My opinion is that we are being robbed right and left somewhere. See that the scales balance, that the girls give exact weight and give the candy and music particular attention. Cut out any old stickers there may be and make leaders of them at a price at which they will go and get the stock into good, clean shape. Music should never pay less than 100% and it has been showing this in the past. On the last report it shows 57.51%

Yours very truly,
E. P. CHARLTON.
Signature dictated.
EPC/MD.

33.

Fall River, Mass.
August 22, 1911.

Mr. Simon Kapstein,
c/o E. P. Charlton Company,
Portland, Oregon.

My dear Kapstein:

Am just in receipt of wire from Mr. Baldwin stating, "Am unable to resume work. Must have time to recover my health. Will be at store frequently to see that all goes right, etc."

Let me know whether Mr. Baldwin has been at the store in the past at all times, or whether he has frequently taken a day or two or three days off. He is getting along in years and no doubt cannot stand the amount of strenuous work that he has in the past.

I am watching the reports daily to see the sales get up where they belong. I hardly think that Mr. Baldwin imagines that you will be able to turn the trick. Now, show them that you are not a "light weight", that you can "eat work" and get this store where it belongs. There is only one thing the matter with it and that is management. It should be doing from $6000.00 to $8000.00 a week and not a dollar less. With the same increase that it has been making for the last five years, it would be in the number one class with Los Angeles, New Orleans and a few of those stores. It is as large a city today as Kansas City and cannot see why not as good. It is doing one-third the business of Kansas City.

Yours truly,

E. P. CHARLTON.
Dictated Signature. EPC/MD.

34.

[September 26, 1911; handwritten on E. P. Charlton & Co., Butte, Mont. letterhead]

Copy of telegram received this morning.

We have placed this matter in the hands of our Mr. Baldwin of Portland with instructions to see Sellars. we shall act accordingly as his advices to us dictate if we find ourselves warranted in so doing shall most certainly arrange settlement to clear up this trouble

E. P. Charlton Co.

35.

[*Handwritten on E. P. Charlton & Co., Butte, Mont. letterhead*]

Butte, Mont.
Sept. 26 1911

Mr. Simon Kapstein
Missoula, Mont.

Dear Mr. Kapstein:-

Your letter received this morning and I was very glad to get it, for it certainly brought good news. I was feeling blue but your letter cheered me. Mr. Williams left yesterday afternoon at 3 o'clock. The sheriff played a mean trick, he said they would leave at 7 o'clock, and that he could come to the store and get his suit case before he left; instead of doing that he sneaked him off at 3 o'clock wouldn't let him see me or get his suit case, so I sent it c/o Mr. Baldwin. Papa went down to the train but could not find him, he must of hid him somewhere. The sheriff was afraid we were going to start something else to hold him here, longer. he was mad to think he had to stay as long as he did.

Mr. Noyes wrote to the Lodge at Portland and told them to do all that they could for him, the Butte Lodge were back of him, and the telegram I got from Charlton Co. this morning, shows that every thing will be alright.

We have 1500 lbs of china at the depot broken to pieces, am sending down barrells & boxes to bring it up to the store and then have the inspector see it, let me know if I am doing right and what else to do.

No one is here yet to take charge of the store but will try and keep every thing straight till some one arrives. Will send your letter to Jack as soon as I find out where he is.

Hoping to have an answer from you soon.

I remain
Yours very truly
Mrs. R. J. Williams

36.

Fall River, Mass.
September 27, 1911.

Mr. Simon Kapstein,
c/o E. P. Charlton & Co.,
Missoula, Mont.

Dear Simon:

I am in receipt of your numerous letters, and glad to know that you are to open next Saturday.

As soon as this store can be conveniently left, say Tuesday or Wednesday, and if Gardner is competent to manage it, you must go down to Butte, and stay there until further notice, and thoroughly investigate this Williams' episode.

He has been extradicted, and is now in jail in Portland under $1500.00 cash bonds. If he is worthy of assistance, we wish to help him in any reasonable way we can, but it looks as though the other side had a good story, and all that he has done is illegal or else there is no justice in Montana. If he has done the thing as alleged he is a natural born crook, and we do not want him in our business. I feel very sorry for his wife, and if she is still in the Butte store and doing well we want to assist her by allowing her to remain there.

However, it would be a temptation for her or any one else in the present case to handle any of our funds. It seems strange that Butte has had such a series of incompetent managers which have cost us money, and I should be delighted to see someone put in that store who could bring it up in the class that I know it should stand.

Let me hear from you as soon as you arrive there.

Yours very truly,
E. P. CHARLTON. Dic. Sig. MAM.

37.

Fall River, Mass.
October 2, 1911.

Mr. S. Kapstein,
c/o Missoula, Mont.

My dear Simon,

Yours received and noted.

Would it be inquisitive to ask what this Five hundred dollar check you received was for, and what the gentleman was in need of so much ready cash after the income he has received for a number of years, and what you think he is doing with this money? I think he is probably correct in his assumption that he will be out of a job January 1st, but if he opens up for himself he certainly will drop what little he has left. I am not satisfied at all with this management, and I believe there have been crooked things going on there for some time, and I am exceedingly sorry that a young man with the opportunity he has had would throw it away. I was told previously to employing him that he was not trustworthy, but I did not take any stock in the information given me.

I congratulate you on a very nice opening. If the store can keep up a business [*crossed out*: like; *in MS*: per week that] it did on the opening day, it will be a winner.

You no doubt have heard that Williams is going back to Butte again. I think I will give the fellow a show until January 1st at least, though there is no doubt but what he has laid himself liable to law, and has not been honest in his business methods. The authorities may have been overbearing and not been able to make out a case--this does not, however, prove him innocent by any means.

Yours very truly,
E. P. CHARLTON.
Dictated Signature. DIC. E. P.C.

38.

Butte, Montana
10/9/1911

Mr. E. P. Charlton
Fall River, Mass.

My Dear Mr. Charlton:

I arrived in Butte at one o'clock Sunday noon. Before seeing Williams I made arrangements to have an interview with the Master of the Masonic Lodge, who told me all he knew of Williams' case. Also saw the Secretary of the same lodge, who told me a like story.

I afterward made arrangements for an appointment with his attorney, and all seemed to agree that Mr. Seller & Co. had no case against Williams. Baker County, Oregon, refused to indict Williams, they having given him a clear title in bankruptcy; but Multnomah County, in which Portland is located, and M. Sellers having quite a lot of influence there and Williams not being personally known there, issued the indictment. Therefore upon presenting the requisition to the Lieut. Governor of Montana, he, the Lieutenant, through courtesy to the Governor of Oregon, signed the requisition.

The basis upon which Mr. Seller placed their case is that Williams neglected to put in three of his assets in filing his papers; one for $500, which he borrowed from his uncle; one for $200 which he borrowed from a friend of his; and $475 which he owed M. Seller & Co.

The attorney only told me in spite of all this they had no legal ground on which to base their case, and that they intended to push the case to a finish and make M. Seller & Co. pay heavily for it.

Personally I think that M. Seller & Co., after finding out that Williams was working for us and that he, only being a boy, they would take legal steps to scare him, and they wrote Williams several threatening letters; whereupon Williams, rather than obtain the notoriety, offered a settlement of $50 a month until the full amount was cleared up, which the boy should never have done.

M. Seller, on the other hand, when he received his letter, in my opinion noticed that Williams was "taking water" and pressed him for the total amount in one payment, which of course Williams could never do, as he hadn't any money to do it with.

I personally feel now, after holding conversations with several of the gentlemen who were interested in the case, that M. Seller will eventually try to drop the case in order to protect himself. Personally I lay all the confidence in the world in Williams and find both him and his wife very faithful to the work and trustworthy, and am quite sure that not a cent of our money has been touched. I furthermore think that no man, under local conditions, can run this store as economically as Williams does. The store looked pretty good, although the shelf trims are the same, in many instances, as those I put up last May. The stock room is pretty much piled up with import and domestic goods, which had accumulated in Willimas' absence. He still has a very heavy stock, and I will try to relieve him a little of it by shipping some down to the Missoula store.

Mrs. Williams, poor girl, is worked to the limit and is almost worn out. The boy is anxious to make good, and feel for the interests of our Company, that the showing this store will make, will be equal to any in our career in business in Butte. I gave him a good, stiff talking to before his wife and uncle and somehow I take a liking to the boy and I above all would be greatly disappointed if he fails to make good. I hardly think it necessary for me to put in any great length of time here, as everything seems to be running smoothly and I will no doubt plan to return to Missoula not later than Thursday.

Yours very truly,
[Simon Kapstein]

39.

Butte, Montana
Oct. 10, 1911

Mr. E. P. Charlton
Fall River
Mass.

My dear Mr. Charlton:

Following up my letter of the 8th inst., I have inquired of local attorneys in regard to Williams' case, and they inform me that M. Seller & Co. can in no way do Williams an injustice, they having accepted their pro rata share in settlement, it is time the stock was closed up.

While here in Butte I have inquired of several men who are familiar with Montana, as to the possibilities of Great Falls and Billings, and from what information I am able to obtain, both of these towns are very good.

While Great Falls is as strong as labor town as Butte is, yet I think if we were able to obtain a 30x100 location there we could make it pay. In addition to the smelters which are located at Great Falls, they have a valuable asset in agricultural and farming produces; and yet while Great Falls is a trifle larger than Missoula, I feel that we could do almost as much business there as we are doing in Butte.

Are you intending to do anything about getting into Cheyenne, Wyoming? That would strike me as being a very good town. I understand a party opened up a store in Sheridan, Wyoming, a town of 6,000, and his opening day sales were $700.

A traveling salesman informed me that Woolworth at Denver had a car load of alarm clocks shipped in, to sell at 15 cents. What truth there is to it I know not.

I am planning on leaving Butte Wednesday night for Missoula, as everything here is running along nicely.

Sincerely yours,
[Simon Kapstein]

40.

Fall River, Mass.
October 17, 1911.

Mr. Simon Kapstein,
c/o The E. P. Charlton & Co.,
 Missoula, Mont.

My dear Simon,

It is our intention to allow you to return to Portland just as soon as you feel it perfectly safe to leave Missoula. If the Aberdeen store is not opened by that time you can leave Missoula and go right there and open this store with Arnott, leaving him in perfect shape, and then return to Portland.

Also, stop off at Spokane and Tacoma. Things look very suspicious and bad to me in Spokane. Cannot understand how business could have gone backwards as it has without something being wrong with the management.

Yours very truly,
E. P. CHARLTON.
Steno.2.
Dic.Sig.

41.

Fall River, Mass.
November 8, 1911.

Mr. Simon Kapstein,
c/o The E. P. Charlton & Co.,
 Portland, Ore.

My dear Simon,

I practically had Mr. Peckham, who is a brother of Frank Peckham, shipped to Portland this week, but on account of the new consolidation have decided to hold him here for the present, as he is a valuable man and will be worth far more to us at this particular time. He is bright, intelligent, and will be capable of filling any store we have. Your brother is also doing well at the store.

Now, my idea is that you and Stevenson leave for Spokane next Sunday, the 19th. You return to Portland the following Thursday or Friday night. Put in all the work you can with all hands, night and day, to get this store in shape. I will write Mr. Files the following letter,--that the entire control of the office is to be turned over to Mr. Stevenson, and his ideas carried out for the balance of the year, that it is our intention to assist him to put this store on its feet if it can be done.

I am very much disturbed, Simon, over the condition of affairs in Spokane. I believe that this man has pulled the wool over your eyes,--that he is a smooth article, and possibly not to be trusted. Many things have come up which are of a suspicious nature,--his trade dropping off as it has,--letters of the kind which I enclose you from Crowther and which please return to this office. Without a doubt Spokane should be doing as much business as last year.

 I believe the money or cash is going somewhere else. I want Stevenson to find out whether or not every register is accurate. Start off his book the day he gets there. Put in a new girl in the office. Mr. Files is to discontinue the services of Mrs. Files as far as that position is concerned.

Tell him not to antagonize him in any way, but to try with all his might to get this business where it should be. Further, goods at the right prices, attractive counters, goods nicely displayed,--that a great deal depends on his future what he can do with this store in assisting to get it back where it should be. At the same time we will know that the business we do from now on is in the treasury.

See that these instructions are carried out to the letter.

Show this enclosed letter & instructions to Mr. Baldwin and talk matters over with him, and I think that he will agree with you that this is the correct procedure. This will allow you to return to Portland and help him out during the heavy holiday inventory.

Yours very truly,
[*signed*] E. P. CHARLTON.
Steno.2.

[*In MS*: Enclose Letter to Mr. Files]

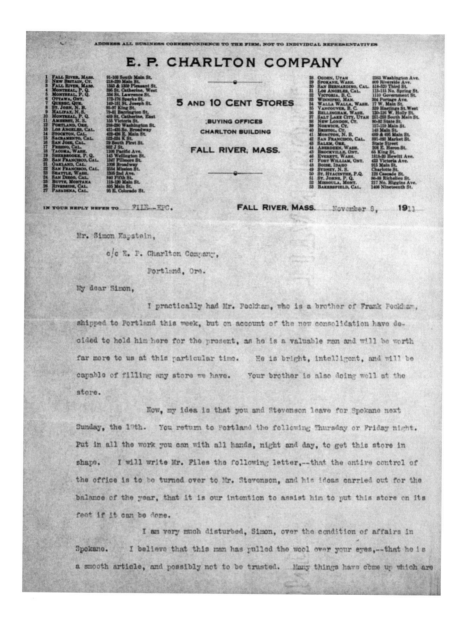

Fig. 25. Document 41, page 1, November 8, 1911. Note that all fifty-three stores are listed on the letterhead.

42.

Fall River, Mass.
February 8, 1912.

Mr. Simon Kapstein,
c/o The E. P. Charlton & Co.,
Portland, Oregon.

Dear Mr. Kapstein,

As you no doubt know, Mr. Charlton is ill, and unable to take up these various matters which he knows more about than does the writer. In any event, I have had a check drawn for the difference between what you have withdrawn during the year and an amount equal to that received by you last year, which I believe will be entirely in accord with Mr. Charlton's wishes. Should there be any change from this, after his convalescence, and he takes these matters in hand, you will hear from him further.

In the meantime, we wish you the best of success under the new management.

Yours very truly,
E. P. CHARLTON COMPANY
BY [*signed*] E. A. Bardol
    V.P.
MD

43.

Portland, Oregon.
February 19th, 1912.

Mr. H. W. Stephenson,
c/o The E. P. Charlton & Co.,
Spokane, Wash.

My dear Stephenson:-

I wish a personal favor, that you would try to find out more about Mr. File's connection with the Palm Confectionary Co. of North Yakima, and write me by return mail. Furthermore I am going to ask you once again if I can be assured of your confidence, that no one will get to know of this. I shall write you upon receiving your reply, of this very peculiar affair.

As to your welfare for this coming year, I will do my level best to see that you are taken care of. You need have no fear that your position is at stake, as your work under my supervision has been all that anyone could ask. I can assure you that if all men we had worked as conscientiously as you have, would be deserving of something better.

With kind regards to Marie, the boy, and yourself, I beg to remain,

Your sincere friend,
S.K.
G.C.

44.

[In MS above E. P. Charleton & Co., Aberdeen, Wash. letterhead: Return]

Aberdeen, Wash.
April 4, 1912.

Mr. W. J. Rand,
San Francisco, Calif.

Dear Sir:-

After two weeks of total silence it sound[*in MS*: s] good to hear a few of the many saw mill whistles. I understand that five of the nineteen mills in town are now running with one-half crew and that in the next two weeks they will all be running. Hope so anyway.

I re-trimmed both windows, making a good heavy display of candy, easter toys, cards and booklets in one window and children's straw hats ladies and misses undervests and ladies, gents and children's hosiery, ladies and gents neckwear, ribbons, jewelry, ladies hair ornaments, laces and other miscellaneous items appropriate for Easter. It seems to me that it would be best here for us to hire a good boy, so that Mr. Arnot might be relieved of some of his work and give trade more attention. As it is now he is trying to do it all himself, and everything is suffering by his so doing. He does his own office work and it suffers in this way that he is compelled to leave it to do on Sunday. It strikes me that while the store might be under a heavy expense by having and $8. or $9. a week boy for the time being, I feel that it would be only a matter of a short time and that it would more than pay us in many different ways. I think the only way to increase our trade, which should never be under $500. a week is to relieve [*in MS*: Mr.] Arnot[*in MS*: t] of some of his work. This I think can be done. It may take a month or two to do it but it [*in MS*: "it" *changed from* "is"; will] eventually [*crossed out*: bound to] come. As it is now, he is in the stock room and office most of the time when he should be watching his trade. I hope to have the stock room in good shape by Monday and if necessary will work Sunday to do it. Changes in the store have all been carried out and completed.

Hoping to hear from you by return mail, I beg to remain,

Very truly yours,
[Simon Kapstein]

45.

May 23, 1912.

Mr. H. P. Hermance,
Care F. W. Woolworth Co.,
San Francisco, Cal.

My dear Mr. Hermance:

Acknowledging receipt of your letter of May 15th, which was forwarded to me from the Aberdeen store. I wish to state that I am positive that I took the electric lamps out of the Salt Lake store window, and boxed them carefully up. Shortly afterwards, the Intermountain Electric Lamp Co.'s man came down and took them away in a one-horse rig. You were at that time talking to Mr. Fosberg, who was then Manager of the Intermountain Electric Lamp Co., right near the Candy counter, and most likely Mr. Fosberg saw his man take them away.

I trust that this will give you the desired information, and beg to remain,

Yours very truly,
[Simon Kapstein]

46.

[LAST WILL AND TESTAMENT]

BE IT KNOWN that I, EARLE P. CHARLTON, of Fall River, Massachusetts, being of sound and disposing mind and memory, do hereby make this my Last Will and Testament, hereby expressly revoking any and all Wills by me at any time heretofore made.

FIRST — I direct the payment by my Executor hereinafter named, of all my just debts and burial charges, and that they shall assume and carry out all legal and moral obligations which I may have heretofore assumed.

SECONDLY — I give to my beloved wife, IDA S. CHARLTON, all sums of money which may stand to my credit a deposit subject to checking account in any national bank or trust company, up to the amount of One hundred thousand dollars ($100,000.00), in the aggregate, same to be hers from and after the date of my decease, after checks already issued by me have been cashed.

THIRDLY — I give to my beloved wife, IDA S. CHARLTON, for and during the term of her natural life or until they are sold by my Trustees, as is hereinafter provided, all my land and buildings on Rock Street, in said Fall River, in that pat of Westport, Massachusetts, known as Acoaxet, and in Palm Beach, in the State of Florida, together with their several appurtenances, furnishings, furniture, equipment and effects, including also all of my stables and garages, the land on which they stand and their customary contents.

I hereby empower my wife and the Trustees names in Article Eleventh of this Will, or their successors, if and whenever they hall deem it advisable, to sell any of said real estate and appurtenances, etc., and to execute, acknowledge and deliver proper deeds and other instruments conveying the same in fee simple to the purchaser or purchasers thereof. The proceeds from each such sale or sales shall be separately held and separately invested and the income thereof shall be disposed of in the manner provided in the Eighth clause of this Will for the disposition of the income of the trust therein set forth.

Upon the death of my wife I give and devise said real estate and appurtenances, etc., then remaining, and the principal of the proceeds of the respective parcels if sold, as follows: My Fall River residence, together with its garage, appurtenances, furniture, furnishing and equipment (including an automobile) to my daughter, VIRGINIA CHARLTON LINCOLN. My Westport Harbor (Acoaxet) estate, with its appurtenances, furniture, furnishings and equipment, stables and garages and their customary equipment (including automobiles) to my daughter, RUTH CHARLTON MITCHELL, and if she should be deceased, to my daughter, VIRGINIA CHARLTON LINCOLN. It is my desire that all of my children shall be entitled to enjoy the Acoaxet property if they so desire, and hope that some amicable arrangement can be made so that each one can occupy it for a season or a part of a season. The Palm Beach property shall, after my wife's death, be held and disposed of a part of the trust set forth in Article Tenth of the Will, with full power of sale and disposition of said real estate to the Trustees and their successors.

FOURTHLY — I make the following specific bequests, to be paid by my Executor within one year from the date of my decease, viz:

These bequests to be paid in cash or its equivalent in stocks, bond or other securities at the discretion of the Executors.

To each of my children, if living,
> EARLE PERRY CHARLTON, JR.,
> RUTH CHARLTON MITCHELL,
> VIRGINIA CHARLTON LINCOLN,

the sum of One hundred thousand dollars ($100,000.00).

To each of my grand-children, in trust with the First National Bank of Boston, interest and principal to be paid them on their twenty-fifth birthday, the sum of Twenty-five thousand dollars ($25,000.00). If any grand-child be deceased before the arrival of his or her aid birthday, the sum provided for him or her to be divided equally among any living grand-children on the twenty-fifth birthday of the deceased grandchild.

To my sister, MARY C. BARDOL, if living, and to my brother JOHN HOWARD CHARLTON, if living, the sums of Twenty-five thousand dollars ($25,000.00) each.

To my brother-in-law, DR. ULYSSES B. STEIN, of Buffalo, if living, Twenty-five thousand dollars ($25,000.00). If deceased, to his wife, if living, and to his children if she shall be dead.

To my sister-in-law, LOUISE S. NEWTON, if living, the sum of Ten thousand dollars ($10,000.00).

To my nieces, SYLVIA CHARLTON, DOROTHY CHARLTON and ELIZABETH CHARLTON, if living, the sum of Ten thousand dollars ($10,000.00) each.

To my nephew, HOWARD BARDOL, if living, the sum of Ten thousand dollars ($10,000.00).

To my nephew, CHARLTON E. LYMAN, if living, the sum of Twenty-five thousand dollars ($25,000.00).

To my loyal and efficient secretary, MARY A. DUNNE, if living, the sum of Twenty-five thousand dollars ($25,000.00).

To ARTHUR S. PHILLIPS, if living, the sum of Ten thousand dollars ($10,000.00).

To my chauffeur, GEORGE F. DONNELLY, if living, the sum of Ten thousand dollars ($10,000.00).

To my most loyal and efficient domestic help, if living and in my employ-
> ANNA McGILLIVRAY — LOUISE CARLSON — ANNA McDONOUGH —
> LOUIS E. PERINI and GEORGE COOK,

the sum of Five thousand dollars ($5,000.00) each.

To the following, if living, and in my employ—
> FRANK SANFORD — JAMES PIERCE — GEORGE COWEN —JAMES DAVIS,

the sum on One thousand dollars ($1,000.00) each.

To all other members of my domestic household who are in my employ at the time of my death and have been so employed for two years or more, the sum of Two hundred dollars ($200.00) each.

No mention is made of my superintendent, GEORGE L. TRIPP, or ALFRED MESSIER, who have already been provided for.

To the following loyal employees of the Quequechan Club, if living,—

MAURICE A. REAGAN — WILLIAM F. BRENNAN — WILLIAM F. KENNEY — FRANK MAYO,

the sum of One thousand dollars ($1,000.00) each.

To the CENTRAL CONGREGATIONAL CHURCH of Fall River, Massachusetts, the sum of Twenty-five thousand dollars ($25,000.00).

To the BOYS CLUB of Fall River, Massachusetts, the sum of Twenty-five thousand dollars ($25,000.00).

To the YOUNG MEN'S CHRISTIAN ASSOCIATION of Fall River, Massachusetts, the sum of Twenty-five thousand dollars ($25,000.00).

To the HOME FOR THE AGED, Fall River, Massachusetts, the sum of Ten thousand dollars ($10,000.00).

To the CHILDREN'S HOME, Fall River, Massachusetts, the sum of Ten thousand dollars ($10,000.00).

To the ST. VINCENT'S ORPHAN HOME, Fall River, Massachusetts, the sum of Ten thousand dollars ($10,000.00).

To the NINTH STREET DAY NURSERY, Fall River, Massachusetts, the sum of Ten thousand dollars ($10,000.00).

To the ST. JOHN'S DAY NURSERY, Fall River, Massachusetts, the sum of Five thousand dollars ($5,000.00).

To the DISTRICT NURSING ASSOCIATION, Fall River, Massachusetts, the sum of Twenty-five thousand dollars ($25,000.00).

FIFTHLY — I devise and bequeath to the TRUESDALE HOSPITAL of Fall River, Massachusetts, the sum of One hundred thousand dollars ($100,000.00), to be applied to the cancellation of debts accrued previous to the first of January, Nineteen hundred and twenty-six, if such there be.

SIXTHLY — I give to the CITY OF FALL RIVER, the sum of Two thousand dollars ($2,000.00), the income of which is to be used for the perpetual care and maintenance of my mausoleum and burial lot in Oak Grove Cemetery.

THE CHARLTON CHARITY TRUST.

SEVENTHLY — Whereas I have deposited with the First National Bank of Boston—Trust Department—Ten thousand (10,000) shares of F. W. Woolworth Co. Common Stock, at a nominal value as of to-day of Two million dollars ($2,000,000.00), and whereas it is my intention to leave this stock in their custody during my natural life, or the proceeds of any sale that shall be made of this stock in the meantime, and I will and direct that at my death, it shall become a permanent trust fund to provide for the following charities and be set aside by said Bank and divided up in the following separate trust, as follows - -

One-quarter of the total, but in no instance to be less than Five hundred thousand dollars ($500,000.00), to be put aside and invested, the income from same to be paid semi-annually to the TRUESDALE HOSPITAL of Fall River, Massachusetts.

One-third of the balance to be set aside as the E. P. CHARLTON FUND, the income to be paid to TUFTS COLLEGE, and to be applied for research work and in the medical department of this institution only, for fellowships and special study that will improve the general standard of the medical department of this institution.

One-half of the then remaining balance to be set aside in another fund, to be known as the IDA S. CHARLTON FUND, income to be paid to the UNION HOSPITAL of Fall River, Massachusetts.

The balance of this fund to be set aside as a separate E. P. CHARLTON FUND, and one-half of the income to be paid semi-annually to the HARRIET LANE HOME department of JOHNS HOPKINS HOSPITAL, Baltimore, Maryland, and the other one-half of the income to the FALL RIVER DISTRICT NURSING ASSOCIATION.

THE CHARLTON BUILDING TRUST.

EIGHTHLY — Whereas I am the owner of three parcels of real estate with the buildings thereon, one on South Main Street, in Fall River, Massachusetts, one on St. Catherine Street West, in Montreal, Canada, and a third on Broadway, in Los Angeles, California, which said three buildings are leased to the F. W. Woolworth Co. for a long term of years, Now, Therefore, I devise the three parcels of land and the buildings aforesaid, together with all the rents and income reserved by or which may arise from or on account of aid leases, and in addition to these three parcels and building, rents and income, I also devise Twenty thousand (20,000) shares of the Common Stock of the F. W. Woolworth Co. to the Trustees named in the Eleventh clause of this Will, same to be known as the CHARLTON BUILDING TRUST.

The income of said fund, or such part of it as my wife, IDA S. CHARLTON, shall request or be in need of, shall be paid to my said wife for and during the term of her natural life, and the balance hall be accumulated and invested by my said Trustees so long as my said wife shall live. After her decease the income of the trust fund shall be divided into three parts, and one part shall be paid to each of my children for and during the term of their natural lives, and after their decease, to their respective children until the youngest child of any of them shall reach the age of twenty-one years. It is my desire that the Trustees shall keep said Woolworth stock intact unless in their unanimous opinion it seems advisable to invest it in other securities, and it shall not be a reason for said sale and reinvestment that said stock has considerable enhanced in market value. If any reinvestments are made by them, they must be made in securities which are at the time allowed to be purchased by the savings banks of the Commonwealth of Massachusetts.

If any of my children shall decease, leaving issue, such issue shall be entitled to his or her parent's share of aforesaid income, and if any child of mine shall decease, leaving no issue, then the husband or wife of such child of mine, provided the person who then may be such husband or wife is in being at the date of my death, shall be entitled to one-third of the income which would be payable to my said child if he or she were living, but such sums payable to the wife or husband of any child of mine shall be only for and during the term of his or her natural life. The remaining two-thirds of such income shall go to my surviving children and the issue of any deceased child in the same manner as other income of the trust is devised. In case any of said income shall be payable to the issue of my children and such issue shall then be under the age of twenty-one years, then my said Trustees shall pay over to such issue, or for their benefit, during said period of minority, only such portion of the income herein provided for as may be necessary for their comfortable support and maintenance, and the unpaid portion shall be invested and accumulated until said issue shall reach the age of twenty-one years. This trust shall terminate when the youngest child of any children of mine shall reach the age of twenty-one years and shall then be divided pro-rata among my next of kin then living as though I deceased at that time. If on account of the laws of any State or Country in which real estate devised under this clause of my Will is situate the term of this trust is directed to be for a longer period of time than shall be allowed by the law of aid State or Country, then as to said real estate the trust shall terminate and division as aforesaid shall be made at the end of the period which under such law is the extreme period allowed thereby, but in no event longer than the period which is hereinabove directed, and in the event of any such termination, I select as the lives designated to determine aid trust in that event and in the following order: First, the life of my wife, second, the life of my youngest child living at my death, third, the life of the youngest child of any children of mine living at my death.

NINTHLY — I direct that any inheritance taxes properly chargeable to any devisee or legatee on account of devises or bequests made under this Will shall be paid by my Executors from my estate.

RESIDUE TRUST.

TENTHLY — All the rest, residue and remainder of my estate, real, personal or mixed, wherever situate or however described, I give to my Trustees hereinafter named, absolutely and in fee simple, but *in trust nevertheless,* to control, hold, manage and invest the same until the death of my said wife, and thereafter until my youngest child shall arrive at the age of thirty-five years, and I empower my said Trustees to invest and reinvest the principal and income thereof in such manner, and in such securities as to them may seem expedient, and they shall not be personally liable for any error of judgment or discretion. I desire, however, that in the making of investments, they follow the general policy I have outlined in a memorandum which is enclosed with this Will. The income of said trust shall be paid to my wife, IDA S. CHARLTON, during her natural life. At her death, the income is to be paid to each of my living children in equal amounts until the youngest child arrives at the age of thirty-five years, when this trust shall terminate.

Upon termination of this trust, I give, devise and bequeath my remaining estate, and I also give, devise and bequeath any property not otherwise disposed of by this Will, equally—one-third to my son; one-third to each of my said daughters. In case any child shall be deceased without issue, I give all of his or her share equally to the survivors, if deceased with issue, such issue shall take the parent's share equally.

ELEVENTHLY — I nominate and appoint the FIRST NATIONAL BANK OF BOSTON, Massachusetts, my wife, IDA S. CHARLTON, and my daughter, VIRGINIA CHARLTON LINCOLN, to be the Executors and Trustees of and under this, my Last Will and Testament, and I request that they shall, in all capacities relating to or growing out of my estate, be exempt from furnishing surety or sureties upon any joint or several official bond, and I nominate and appoint said MARY A. DUNNE to be the Secretary of said Executors and Trustees, and direct them to pay her for her services to both at the rate of Five thousand dollars ($5,000.00) per annum. Further, it is a condition of each of the legacies named in this Will (which term shall include the payments made in the final distribution of my estate) that payments thereof shall, in the descretion of my said Executors or Trustees, be made either in cash or in securities of equivalent market value on the date when such payments are made.

Further, in case of the death, resignation or incapacity of either or any of said Executors or Trustees, my daughter, RUTH CHARLTON MITCHELL, or her husband, FREDERICK M. MITCHELL, shall be appointed, and if the FIRST NATIONAL BANK OF BOSTON shall be or become disqualified to act, then an institution named by the surviving Trustees may assume the obligation imposed hereby and shall have all the powers granted hereby and be exempt from furnishing sureties.

IN WITNESS WHEREOF, I have hereunto set my hand and seal this Second day of January, One thousand nine hundred and twenty-six

Earle. P. Charlton (Seal)

Signed, sealed, published and declared by the above-named EARLE P. CHARLTON as and for his Last Will and Testament, in the presence of us, who, in his presence, in the presence of each other, and at his request, have hereunto subscribed our names as witnesses, all this Second day of January, One thousand nine hundred and twenty-six.

Roy Creighton, residing at Malba, N.Y.
Hiram W. Deyo, residing at Monclair, N.J.
P. Hofer, residing at Kew Gardens, N.Y.
Edward Cornell, residing at Central Valley, N.Y.

COMMONWEALTH OF MASSACHUSETTS.

BRISTOL SS.   PROBATE COURT.

I, GUILFORD C. HATHAWAY, Register of the Probate Court for said County of Bristol, having by law the custody of the seal and all the records, books, documents and papers of or appertaining to said Court, hereby certify the paper hereto annexed to be a true copy of a paper appertaining to said Courts, and on file and of record in the office of said Court, to wit: Will of Earle P. Charlton, late of Fall River, in said County.

IN WITNESS WHEREOF, I have hereunto set my hand and the seal of said Court, this   day of
in the year of our Lord one thousand nine hundred and thirty-

Register.